"Paul is one of those prec   y
to act as wise and mature   p
community. As a life-long   ;
created a tsunami of ripples ;   zles
and offers a path for change."

— *STANFORD SIVER, Ph.D., conflict psychology, former Director of Institute for MultiTrack Diplomacy, and co-founder of Deep Democracy Institute*

"Paul Cienfuegos is the Thomas Paine of our time, sounding the alarm about threats to democracy, and reminding us that each of us together has the power to transform our lives and society. *How Dare We? Courageous Practices to Reclaim Our Power as Citizens* is an inspiring collection of must-read pieces as we work to protect what is vital and work toward deep democracy."

— *CHUCK COLLINS, director at Program on Inequality at the Institute for Policy Studies, co-editor of Inequality.org, and author of The Wealth Hoarders: How Billionaires Pay Millions to Save Trillions*

"Paul Cienfuegos is a master at explaining paradigm shifting concepts in a clear and comprehensible way. He then offers effective actions to address the most critical issues of our time. His passion for and commitment to citizen democracy is inspiring. His ability to bring people with disparate views together around shared values provides communities a path to reclaim the power We the People have."

— *LYNDA MCCLURE, retired community and union organizer*

"Do your hopes and desires include making a positive change in the world? This book will inspire you and set you on a path that could save you years, decades, of futile floundering in the labyrinth we call the regulatory process, and give you shovel-ready ideas for creating meaningful and impactful participation in governance and community self-determination."

— *ANN KOBSA, Ph.D., conservationist and subsistence farmer*

"In the almost 20 years I've known Paul Cienfuegos, he's taught me a lot about what can be possible when ordinary citizens become vocal citizens, and towns we live in can change from towns to actual communities … Even so, this collection of essays and talks has grabbed me by surprise. Paul's writing has pulled me in, engaged me in a way few writers do. I've learned critical bits of U.S. and corporate history that are not taught in school, but are so important to every single one of us who cares about how and where we live, who cares about environmental justice, about corporate privilege and government-corporate collusion that deny us, regular people, our constitutional rights … Stories seldom told or explained elsewhere, guaranteed to open your eyes and maybe even inspire you to take action. Thank you, Paul."
— *SARA SUNSTEIN, somatic educator*

"Paul Cienfuegos is one of the very few speakers that we broadcast on Alternative Radio that offers concrete solutions. A remarkably large number of people respond positively to his analyses for that reason."
— *DAVID BARSAMIAN, founder and director of Alternative Radio*

"Paul Cienfuegos has spent many decades working on a wide range of social, political and economic issues, during which time we have had many opportunities to work together. Such issues have existed for a long time and they are all intertwined. I especially like how Paul's work shows no matter the single issue they all lead to a similar conclusion of working locally within our communities becoming strong as We the People. It all really comes down to that. The accessibility is excellent and the consolidation valuable for understanding where this is all going. Paul's willingness to open his heart is a strong incentive for one to read to the finish. We do need to humanize ourselves; trust one another … This is a wonderful project. I am glad Paul has tackled it. Looking forward to more."
— *NANCY HORTON, small farmer and homesteader for 45 years, mom and grandma, weaver, active citizen for 40 years*

"I have known Paul Cienfuegos for 40 years. He was fresh out of college when he experienced an early form of the experiential group process known now as the Work That Reconnects. Immediately recognizing its potential, he acquired the basics of its facilitation before leaving as planned for Scotland. There, in the workshops he began offering, local people felt free to speak out against their government hosting US nuclear missiles and planes, and letting their land be used as target practice and launching pad for President Reagan's campaign against the Soviet Union. By the time I arrived two years later in 1983, Paul's work had grown a network of active groups in towns across Scotland and England. Now, eager to host us, they were recruiting for workshops for us to co-lead. Our unforgettable two-week tour allowed me to see Paul with fresh eyes: I witnessed his efficacy as an organizer, his political smarts and natural warmth, his passion for empowering people, the deep well of his caring. Out of this caring, leadership grew from among the Scottish and English ranks and a national organization took form, called Interhelp UK. Over recent decades, these capacities of Paul's are manifest in Community Rights US. This spunky organization shows communities (towns, counties) how to protect their natural resources from corporate exploitation by knowing and claiming rights they already possess. It is wonderful to know about, and sets me to thinking of the passion for democracy I experienced in Paul Cienfuegos 40 years ago."
— *JOANNA MACY*, author of **World As Lover, World As Self**

"In our complex and fast changing world we need books that not only help us understand the connections between our different problems but also offer solutions that point us towards the future we deserve. Luckily for everyone who cares about making positive change, veteran community organizer and educator Paul Cienfuegos has distilled a lifetime of community organizing wisdom and grassroots campaigns into exactly such a book. He provides everything you need, to leave behind your inner underdog and start tapping into collective power. Don't miss this important guide from one of our foremost experts on community rights and grassroots democracy."
— *PATRICK REINSBOROUGH, founder of the Center for Story-based Strategy, and author of* **Re:Imagining Change: how to use story-based strategy to win campaigns, build movements and change the world**

"I first met Paul 25 years ago when he came to our community to help us learn how the corporate stranglehold on all aspects of our lives was the primary issue to address. We had been addressing environmental damage in the typical whack-a-mole style, running from one problem to another, always desperate to raise more money to have a new legal challenge, constantly begging the regulators to see the damage that was being done to our environment and our communities. Paul opened our eyes and taught us the history we needed to know. He showed us how other communities had successfully prevented the corporate domination of their community.

We were specifically concerned with how we could prevent the corporate timber barons from controlling our local elections. We organized and successfully ran a ballot initiative that prevented financial contributions from outside corporations.

I have read many books written on the environmental destruction and injustice that we as citizens face. But they did not help me understand the big picture and give me concrete solutions I could apply to my community. Paul's clear and concise book shines a light on the whole historical mess and shows us clearly the root of the problem. Identifying the root is essential to creating meaningful and lasting change. This book will help guide you to develop the strategies and solutions you need for your community to repel the corporate domination."

— *GIL GREGORI, riparian restorationist and residential property manager*

"Community Rights organizer-teacher Paul Cienfuegos has arrived in town with a whole lot of very useful, often shocking information you didn't know before and a big load of energy, ideas, experience and inspiration to get you using that information to make some true democracy in your community. But be ready to be influenced, deeply, by Cienfuegos' teaching, and to find your commitment to life-centered change-making energized forever."

— *MATT NICODEMUS, draft resister and war resistance organizer, co-author of* **The Graduation Pledge of Social and Environmental Responsibility,** *co-founder of the Graduation Pledge Alliance, and founder and co-coordinator of Sworn to Refuse*

HOW DARE WE?

Courageous Practices
to Reclaim
Our Power as Citizens

Paul Cienfuegos

HOW DARE WE?
Courageous Practices
to Reclaim
Our Power as Citizens

Paul Cienfuegos

100fires Press
Portland, Oregon

How Dare We?
Courageous Practices to Reclaim
Our Power as Citizens

© 2022 Paul Cienfuegos

Cover photo by David Clode
Contact: @DavidClode

Author: Paul Cienfuegos

ISBN: 978-1-0879-3952-0
To contact the author:
Paul@CommunityRights.US

100fires Press
100fires.com

We wish not to seize power, but to exercise it.

– Subcomandante Marcos, the nom de guerre used by the (once) main spokesperson of the Zapatista Army of National Liberation in Mexico

Our deepest fear is not that we are inadequate. Our deepest fear is that we are powerful beyond measure. It is our light, not our darkness that most frightens us. We ask ourselves, "Who am I to be brilliant, gorgeous, talented, fabulous?" Actually, who are you not to be? You are a child of God. Your playing small does not serve the world. There is nothing enlightened about shrinking so that other people won't feel insecure around you. We are all meant to shine, as children do. We were born to make manifest the glory of God that is within us. It's not just in some of us; it's in everyone. And as we let our own light shine, we unconsciously give other people permission to do the same. As we are liberated from our own fear, our presence automatically liberates others.

– Marianne Williamson,
A Return to Love: Reflections on the Principles of A Course in Miracles

Dedication

I dedicate this book to the following beloveds.

⟶ My parents **Elka and Myron**, who always supported my life choices, even though it was clear that they had wanted me to become a doctor, a lawyer, or a math professor! Thank you for believing in me, through thick and thin!

⟶ **Joanna Macy**, Buddhist scholar, and my first significant mentor. Through a masterful fluke of the universe, I found myself in exactly the right city, Philadelphia, on exactly the right day in 1982 to become a participant at Joanna's first-ever intensive training for workshop leaders. She had only recently created a workshop titled Despair and Empowerment in the Nuclear Age. The workshop, and the social movement that followed, were all about helping people come to terms with their feelings of despair and rage and grief and sorrow about the dire state of our world, rather than going numb and avoiding the topic at all costs.

I literally drove straight from this training to the Boston Airport and flew to England, as an organizer for the British portion of The Walk to Moscow, offering this new workshop to anyone and everyone I met there. Long story short, I ended up living in rural Scotland for three years, led Joanna's workshops dozens of times across Britain and France, and co-founded Interhelp-UK (with Mary Simister, Maria Brown, and many others) which continued doing great work for years after I returned to the United States. Joanna was instrumental in helping to train the Brits who carried on the work there.

Joanna became a lifelong friend and she and I are colleagues in what is now known as The Work That Reconnects. I do not believe that I could have personally sustained 44 years of work focused on social movement without having learned from her how to breathe through my pain for the world and share that breath with all of Mother Earth's other breathers.

"Act your age," Joanna was fond of reminding us, and by that she meant, when Joni Mitchell sang, "We are Stardust," that Joni was literally correct. The very molecules of our bodies were birthed in the Big Bang that created the entire universe. So, we truly are 14 billion years old. Every one of us. Earth needs us to act our age, as wise and mature beings, now more than ever.

—๑ **Jacqueline Mayrand,** my best friend for many years, who has stood with me through many scary and traumatic life moments, who continues to dive deep with me into wild nature as often as possible, and who is equally capable of being held by me as we dance and cry and giggle our way through this miracle of life.

We hold these truths to be self-evident,

that all men are created equal,

that they are endowed by their Creator

with certain unalienable Rights,

that among these are

Life, Liberty and the pursuit of Happiness.

That to secure these rights, Governments are instituted among Men,

deriving their just powers from the consent of the governed,

That whenever any Form of Government

becomes destructive of these ends,

it is the Right of the People to alter or to abolish it,

and to institute new Government,

laying its foundation on such principles and

organizing its powers in such form,

as to them shall seem most likely to effect their Safety and Happiness.

An excerpt from the
Declaration of Independence, July 4, 1776

Table of Contents

Introduction

Ever since I was a teenager in the 1970s, a helluva long time ago, I have tried to live my life as if the world that I wanted to live in was already here. I was an unusual and very intense teenager, not a lot of friends, growing up in an all-white, culturally barren Albuquerque suburb in New Mexico that sprawled endlessly across the desert.

Yearning for a real sense of community around me that wasn't there, I lived as best I could, as if that world had already arrived. That feeling has never gone away. Fortunately, over these many decades since I was young, I have learned a lot about how we humans could actually co-create that healthier society. I am hungry to share some of these stories and visions with you.

My primary goal with this book is to light a fire under you! To convince you that there are obvious achievable solutions for many of our society's most (supposedly) intractable problems and that these solutions require us to re-imagine ourselves as part of an absolutely enormous body of humanity that I choose to describe as We the People, for that is where our ultimate power and authority resides.

We are the decision makers
that we've been waiting for.

We live in a profoundly alienating society. We are taught from a young age to define ourselves as *consumers* and *workers*, that our greatest power is to vote with our dollars, to ally with a political party, and distrust people from other political parties. This is no way to build a genuinely participatory society.

As I have said for many years, conservatives fear big government, while progressives fear the huge corporations that control our government.

These two sides are a lot closer to finding common ground in this scenario than most people realize.

Our most important work at this time is to remember who we are. We are the decision makers that we've been waiting for. Not just as voters from opposing political parties. Not just workers and consumers. But as We the People, as citizens. At least on paper, our nation was designed as a democratic republic, though it has never functioned as one. It is time for us to stand up together and exercise our constitutional authority to govern ourselves, where we live, **to make this democratic republic live up to the ideals that we were taught about in school.**

The essays in this book are here to provoke you, to stretch you, sometimes way beyond your comfort level. The book is full of practical ideas that any caring person can run with. I guarantee you won't be bored!

More than half of this book is written from the perspective of my decades of work in the community rights movement, where people from all ideologies and political parties have been working successfully together to protect the health, safety, and welfare of the communities where each of us lives. In our work, we are constantly having to remind ourselves that **We the People are at the top of the decision-making food chain, at least constitutionally!** We are sovereign people, which means we have the authority to govern ourselves.

I'm ready to help in any way that I can.
Just give me a shout!
I mean this!

Our government is constitutionally required to serve us. It has duties and responsibilities to us. When it fails in those duties, when it ignores the will of the people which it now does every day, consent of the governed is not happening. That is the situation we now find ourselves in. (The same constitutional framework exists between We the People and *our* business corporations, by the way.)

The remaining portions of the book contain a whole variety of project and campaign ideas that I have envisioned over many years. Some of them are still waiting for the right person to come along and grab them by the tail. **Maybe that person is YOU?**

Topics include how to build more effective social movement infrastructure for the longer term. We the People should not have to keep reinventing the wheel decade after decade. This sort of thing drives me mad!

Over the past many decades, I have designed major campaigns and projects from scratch and then done my damnedest to make them real, on the ground, sometimes successfully. As I did from my earliest years, I dream the future I want to live in. Sometimes there isn't yet anyone out there willing to fund these visions. Projects such as these:

- *Salmon Coming Home: A Clayoquot Restoration Camp* was fully designed but never took place, in a specific massive ancient forest clear cut on Vancouver Island in Canada.
  Do you dream of transforming your local corporate clear cut into a grassroots ecological restoration pilot project and teaching extravaganza? Look no further!

- *The Democratic Logging Project* was co-designed by six of us in Humboldt County, California to model how the people of that place could wrest decision-making control away from corporate forest destroyers and place it firmly in the hands of local communities.
  Does your community dream of a future where it takes back decision-making control from large logging corporations? Look no further!

- A Sliding Scale design that anyone can utilize shows how to make conferences, trainings, or gatherings more financially fair to all who wish to attend. This has been successfully put into practice by a number of groups over many years.
  FYI, if you're not charging at least a 5 to 1 sliding scale fee ratio for your event, you're perpetuating the outrageous status quo reality where the lower income attendees are heavily subsidizing the wealthier attendees! Yes, really!

- *An International Campaign to End U.S. Assaults on the World,* which I created over the past decade (pre-Trump) but have never shared with anyone until now. Our planet's peoples and other living beings need it now more than ever.
  Do you have a similar dream? Let's make this happen.

I don't own any of these ideas. We need a big-vision culture shift on the ground. Yours and mine! There is no time for any further delay. I'm ready to help in any way that I can. Just give me a shout! I mean this!

Every single aspect of my life's work has been about one central thing: creating the most peaceful, just, and ecologically sustainable participatory democracy in these disUnited States as rapidly as humanly possible. I have been driven towards this goal with every fiber of my being, for most of my 63 years. I want to see this as a reality so badly! Don't you?!

I am rapidly becoming an elder. I am slowing down; still yearning for a life partner; hiking, backpacking, playing; resting more and more, engaging politically less and less. **This may be my best shot at sharing with the world what I have learned.** Or maybe this is only my first of many books! Who the hell knows? Life is a grand adventure!

Thank you, dear reader, from the bottom of my heart, for giving me this sacred opportunity! Once you have read my book, I so very much look forward to hearing directly from you. I am available to help you think through how you can begin to more boldly exercise your power and authority.

Email me at Paul@CommunityRights.US. You can check out our organization's website at www.CommunityRights.US. Also, please don't miss the slew of additional bonus materials you can access entirely for free, all listed at the end of the book, or directly via www.CommunityRights.US/Book.

Dive in! And remember to breathe!

– Paul Cienfuegos

Chapter One

Let's Start
at the Beginning.
Shall We?

The twentieth century has been characterized by three developments
of great political importance: the growth of democracy, the growth
of corporate power, and the growth of corporate propaganda
as a means of protecting corporate power against democracy.

—*Alex Carey, Australian writer, social psychologist, and sheep farmer,*
from **Taking The Risk Out of Democracy**

Our Government

Doesn't Serve Us ...

By Design

This speech was presented to the people of Decorah, Iowa on September 26th, 2013 and was sponsored by the Community Rights Alliance of Winneshiek County. David Barsamian then broadcast an edited version of it to his nationally syndicated Alternative Radio audience.

I would like to begin my talk tonight with a quote from Wendell Berry, a lifelong farmer and prolific author who has written dozens of books about his unshakeable connection to the land, rural communities, and meaningful work:

> The idea of citizenship in the United States seems to me to have been greatly oversimplified. It has become permissible to assume that ALL one needs to do to become a good citizen ... is to vote ... and obey ... and pay taxes, as if one can be a good citizen without being a citizen either of a community ... or of a place.

What does it mean to be a good citizen in the place where you live? My colleagues and I in the community rights movement have come to believe quite firmly that if we can't practice real democracy in the place where we live, then we can't honestly claim that we live in a democratic society at all.

Think about it. Each of us lives somewhere. We don't live in a country or in a state. We live in a very particular spot on the landscape. Our day-to-day activities take place in that spot on the landscape: in a city, a town, or a rural area.

So, we need to ask ourselves a fundamental question about that spot where each of us lives. **Do we have any real direct authority as a citizen, there, in that place?** Because if we do not, we've all got a problem!

- If the board of directors of a large corporation announces their plan to build a factory farm in your rural county, do most of the people or a majority of the elected officials in your community get to decide yay or nay?

- When Walmart Corporation's directors decide to build yet another store in your community, does the public or its elected officials get to decide whether this will be allowed or not?

- When the federal government announces it is going to build a new superhighway that skirts the edge of your community, do you or your elected officials have a say in whether that happens or not?

- When Nestle Corporation's directors announce they're building a new water bottling plant in your community, do you get to vote on it first? Especially given that water is becoming the new oil, and water that is safe to drink is becoming more and more scarce.

- When your state government gives a fracking corporation a permit to start drilling for so-called "natural" gas at the edge of your town, does your community have the authority to veto the drilling plan before it even starts?

- When fracking operations that are going on all over the United States require an endless supply of a very special and unusual kind of sand (frac sand), as is currently being proposed in Iowa and nearby states, who gets to decide whether your local hills are going to be blown apart to get that sand which will then be transported a thousand miles away? Is it the folks who live in rural Iowa or the directors of those large corporations who couldn't care less about the people who live there?

These are just a few examples of what I mean when I ask you whether real democracy exists in your town or in your county. Do the majority of residents, or a majority of your elected officials, get to have a meaningful say as to whether or not these proposed activities happen in your community or not? **Because if they don't, then we can't reasonably claim that our society operates democratically.**

We can change this! It doesn't have to be this way!

The work that I do as a full-time community organizer and teacher is about helping communities to rethink what is the proper relationship between our governmental institutions and We the People. As community rights organizer Kai Huschke says, "It's about re-engineering what government is about, what government is for." If what is normal in our society is that you and I have virtually no democratic authority over the decisions that affect all of us, then it's time to do something different than what we're used to doing as citizens. That is the work of the community rights movement in which I am active. We're about driving into law new rights of self-governance for communities. **Things only change with pressure from below.** That is where we're doing most of our work. In fact, 160 communities in nine states have already done just that over the past 13 years; they've passed local laws that enshrine local law-making authority and that stop corporate harms before they even happen.

Now some will say, "But communities already have a say. That's what the regulatory process is all about." The regulatory process ensures that before a factory farm, or a big box store, or a water bottling plant is built, the company has to get a permit from the state to build it. Before that can happen, the state (or federal) Department of Agriculture, or the Water Resources Board, or the state energy agency, is required to hold a public hearing so that you can speak your mind. This proves that society is operating democratically. At least that's the claim.

I would argue that just the reverse is true. In each of these examples, the state or federal agency that holds the public hearing does so only because it is required to. But it's normally a foregone conclusion that the project will be approved, even before the public hearing takes place. Why? Because that's how the law works. We the People aren't supposed to know this. It is supposed to be too complicated for dummies like us to understand, but here's what is true: state and federal regulatory agencies rarely deny a permit to a factory farm (or a big box store or a water bottling plant or a proposed clear-cut logging operation or an oil lease or a toxic waste incinerator or a coal fired power plant or a frac sand mining operation), just as long as the proposed activity meets all of the current regulatory requirements. Given that regulatory laws are generally written by the industries which are going to be regulated, the permit is almost always approved. This is how the system operates. It was *designed* this way.

These regulatory agencies were a brilliant invention in the late 1880s. The federal government and the leading corporate executives of the time from the railroad industry met together to create a new body of law called *regulatory law*. The first regulatory agency was the ICC, or Interstate Commerce Commission, established in 1887. Charles Adams, President of the Union Pacific Railroad Company wrote, "What is desired is something having a good sound, but quite harmless, which will impress the popular mind with the idea that a great deal is being done, when in reality, very little is intended to be done."

What were the regulatory agencies actually designed to accomplish? President Cleveland's Attorney General, Richard Olney, explained to railroad corporation executives that the ICC was to be "a sort of barrier between the railroad corporations and the people." The public was to be pacified with laws that sounded tough but placed much discretion in the hands of regulators. Who was put in charge of the regulatory agencies? High-level staff from the very industry that was to be regulated. And who was to write the actual regulations? The same high-level staff from the very industry that was being regulated! In other words, **We the People get to enforce the rules that industry wrote for themselves!**

So, that's the regulatory process that we are funneled into when we share our concerns about plans that corporations have for our communities. Not exactly a process that engenders democratic participation.

Once you know this history, it starts making a heck of a lot more sense why this alphabet soup of state and federal government agencies almost always approves the corporate development they've been asked to approve. So, when I hear concerned citizens complain that the U.S. Department of Agriculture (USDA) has been captured by the agricultural industry, or that the Department of Energy has been captured by the coal and oil industry, or that the Department of Forestry has been captured by the logging industry, I have to both laugh and cry. You see, **none of these industries had to capture these agencies. They already run them, and they always have!** A Monsanto Corporation executive runs the USDA, and so on. This is how the system works. It was *designed* to work this way. We should stop being surprised whenever an agency approves the latest frac sand mining operation, or the latest cell tower, or the latest whatever! It's not ours to decide, they claim. We have virtually no control at all over what happens in our own communities. We just have to grin and bear it. (Editor's note: For a recent real-life example, check out the newspaper OpEd from Iowa State Representative Ralph Watts on page 153.)

If we can't practice real democracy in the place where we live, we really can't honestly claim that we live in a democratic society at all.

But there's more. It gets worse. There is just one avenue for citizen input, the regulatory law system, when a corporation comes to town with a plan that local residents don't like. But that's not all. If our local elected officials try to bypass this system and attempt to pass a local law that prohibits the proposed corporate activity, they get slapped by state government. Why? Because it is actually illegal for them to do so. How can that be?

Here's how. More than a century ago, a judge named John Forrest Dillon, who served on the Iowa Supreme Court from 1862 to 1869, came up with a theory about state governments having complete authority over local governments. The theory came to be known as Dillon's Rule. In an 1868 court case he stated, "Municipal corporations [that means municipal governments] owe their origin to, and derive their powers and rights wholly from, the legislature. It breathes into them the breath of life, without which they cannot exist. As it creates, so may it destroy. If it may destroy, it may abridge and control." In other words, and again I quote, "[M]unicipal governments only have the powers that are expressly granted to them by the state legislature."

Dillon referred to municipalities as "mere tenants … of their respective state legislatures" which could be "eliminated by the legislature with a stroke of the pen."

The U.S. Supreme Court fully adopted Dillon's theory in an 1891 court case, in Merrill v. Monticello. So much for the notion that all power is inherent in the people or that local self-government is a matter of natural right that does not need to be conferred by higher political structures, as many state constitutions either imply or explicitly state.

So, you see, it doesn't actually matter what kind of ideas the local residents may have about the sort of community they wish to live in. They can pull together all of the public processes they want. They can work hard to ensure that the residents of their community get to contribute their best thinking so that an official 20-year or even 50-year plan gets written down and passed by their elected officials, describing in great detail the kind of town or city or environmental protection they have decided to leave for their children and grandchildren. **But ultimately, the state government can treat their municipality as a mere child that it can overrule with the stroke of a pen.**

As I said earlier, we in the community rights movement believe that **if we can't practice real democracy in the place where we live, we really can't honestly claim that we live in a democratic society at all.** So, we're out to change that!

Here's a related quote from Alexis de Tocqueville, a 19th century historian best known for his book, *Democracy in America*. "Without power and independence, a town may contain good subjects but it can contain no active citizens."

So we start from the premise that we in fact do not live in a democratic republic, even though we were all taught in school that we do, because we are currently not allowed to practice real democracy in the places where we live.

Allow me to share another bit of early American history that you may not know. Everything I am about to tell you is verifiable. None of it is conspiracy theory; I promise!

This country has had two national constitutions, not just one. The drafting of our first constitution was completed in 1777 and was ratified by all 13 states in 1781. It was intended as our long-term constitution, but it was illegally thrown out and replaced by our second constitution, the one we have now, in 1789, just 12 years after it had gone into effect.

Our original constitution was titled, The Articles of Confederation and Perpetual Union. It was a profoundly more democratic document than our second constitution. The people of the 13 colonies had not fought in the Revolutionary War against the British monarchs and their empire simply to turn around and create yet another empire that oppressed most of its inhabitants. The vast majority of people in the 13 colonies wanted something very different. They wanted local control over their lives. They wanted some guarantee of liberty and justice for all, regardless of rank or status. With this goal in mind, they wrote a very different constitution than the one we have now. It was a revolutionary constitution. All power was decentralized. The people would have significant self-governing authority in their own communities.

State government would be primary, while federal government would exist mainly to facilitate discussion and coordination between the states.

To make this a reality, federal government had few of the powers it has today. There were no permanent courts. **There was no Supreme Court that could overrule the will of the people or its elected representatives.** There was no U.S. Senate, which today is equivalent to Britain's House of Lords; in other words, a millionaire's club. There was only the Congress of the Confederation, the place where the representatives from each state gathered to discuss issues of national significance. The Congress of the Confederation could make decisions, but the implementation of those decisions, including modifications to the constitutional document itself, required unanimous approval of all 13 state legislatures.

There was no standing army, nor could the national government establish one. Only the states had the authority to create militias to respond to specific threats to their security, and these militias were only temporary. Nine of the 13 states had to agree before the Confederation could engage in a war. And finally, **there was no executive branch: no single person could rule over everyone else.**

Quoting from the document itself, "Each state retains its sovereignty, freedom, and independence, and every power, jurisdiction, and right, which is not by this Confederation expressly delegated."

We were all taught in school that the brilliance of our republic is the checks and balances between the executive branch, the legislative branch, and the judicial branch. Yet our first constitution, which was much more democratic than our current constitution, provided only one of these branches: the Congress. **Is it possible that even the checks and balances that we were taught about in school have a very different purpose than what we were told?** Is it possible that instead, these separate elements of government were designed to make it supremely difficult for We the People to pass laws that we favored, because the Senate or the Executive or the Supreme Court could ultimately veto the desires of the majority?

The wealthiest and most influential members of this early society did not favor such a decentralized form of government, where the individual states held the primary political power. They, in fact, did wish to build a new empire, but with themselves in the lead. So, they began to actively work towards getting rid of the Articles of Confederation and Perpetual Union.

They replaced them with something that flipped the government upside down, with a strong federal government that ruled over the states.

Here's a description of what took place, in the words of Richard Henry Lee, writing in *The Federal Farmer*:

> The idea of destroying ultimately, the state government, and forming one consolidated system, could not have been admitted—a convention, therefore, merely for vesting in congress power to regulate trade was proposed ... September 1786, a few men from the middle states met at Annapolis, and hastily proposed a convention to be held in May, 1787, for the purpose, generally, of amending the confederation ... still not a word was said about destroying the old constitution, and making a new one. ... The States still unsuspecting, and not aware that they were passing the Rubicon, appointed members to the new convention, for the sole and express purpose of revising and amending the confederation—and, probably, not one man in ten thousand in the United States, till within these 10 or 12 days, had an idea that the old ship was to be destroyed ...

Now, for the first time in our nation's history, 13 years after the nation was founded, we would have our first president, George Washington. Now, state and federal courts would be established, along with the Supreme Court, which could overrule the people's laws. Now, a second branch of the legislature, the Senate, would be established. Now, state authority would be trumped by federal authority.

And they call this democracy?!

We ended up with a constitution that is all about the rights of property and says almost nothing about the rights of people.

When the people living in the 13 states found out what had been done in Philadelphia behind locked doors, the response in almost every state was pure outrage. Here's just one example from the historical record. Amos Singletary, a local farmer, is recorded as having made the following statement in Sutton, Massachusetts:

These lawyers, and men of learning, and moneyed men, that
talk so finely, and gloss over matters so smoothly, to make us,
poor illiterate people, swallow down the pill, expect to get into
Congress themselves; they expect to be the managers of this
Constitution, and get all the power and all the money into
their own hands, then they will swallow up all us little folks,
like the great leviathan.

The states ultimately refused to ratify the new constitution because it spoke only of the rights of property and commerce. Nowhere in the second constitution was there mention of rights for people. So, those who had written it were forced to promise that a series of amendments would be added later that guaranteed certain rights to all people, and this promise was sufficient to get the states to finally ratify it. We call the first ten amendments of our second constitution, The Bill of Rights. Most of us think these amendments were all part and parcel of the original document because we have a flattened understanding of our own history.

The official myth of our nation's founding is about liberty and justice for all. Sadly, this was never intended to exist in reality, at least not after our second constitution was drafted.

James Madison was the primary architect of our second constitution. He spoke quite explicitly at the Constitutional Convention in Philadelphia about his vision for government. Here's one of the things he said, the primary goal of government is "to protect the minority of the opulent against the majority."

I'll read that again, because it's critical for us to understand why our system of government operates the way it does.

James Madison, the primary architect of our second constitution, stated at the Constitutional Convention in Philadelphia, that the primary goal of government is "to protect the minority of the opulent against the majority." And his colleague John Jay was fond of saying, "The people who own the country ought to govern it."

So, it's no surprise that our second constitution, the one that we now live under, is all about property and commerce, and almost entirely not about the rights of people. This is because the folks who wrote it were really most interested in designing a nation state where those with the most property got to rule. Those with little or no property (which has always been the vast majority of us) got laws that look democratic on the surface but which actually exclude most of us from full participation. We merely give input to those in charge. We ended up with a constitution that is all about the rights of property and says almost nothing about the rights of people. This was the vision of James Madison and George Washington. The only reason that we even have a Bill of Rights is that the public didn't like the second constitution at all and demanded that amendments be added that were explicitly about rights.

By the way, I'm not asking you to believe my history lesson. If you're at all skeptical, check it out. Do your own research.

> *State control of cities, then, may be regarded*
> *as a means of protecting the local minority*
> *against the local majority.*

Let's return for a few minutes to the American Revolution, and for this I'm going to quote substantially from Ben Price, the Projects Director at the Community Environmental Legal Defense Fund.

> **The American Revolution was primarily about local self-government.** Revolutionary colonists were adamantly opposed to what they referred to as a "ministerial" form of government, where all decisions affecting their communities were made in advance by the central government. Those local leaders appointed by their British superiors were only given the authority to administer the laws set forth from above, and no authority to make their own. This procedural denial of rights was unacceptable to the colonists, so they began to write local "declarations of independence" to prepare for separation from the king. Historian Pauline Maier has documented over 90 Declarations of Independence issued by community governments throughout the colonies in the spring and summer of 1776. It was these expressions of frustration with the central government, and their complaints that necessary laws were being pre-empted by the servants of the empire, that inspired Thomas Jefferson's more famous *Declaration of Independence* in 1776. There's much more to learn about this story in Pauline Maier's book, *American Scripture: Making the Declaration of Independence.*

Most of us haven't read the Declaration of Independence since we were kids. It's quite a remarkable document and I urge you to have another look. The Declaration includes a long list of reasons why the colonists no longer owed allegiance to the British Empire. The first complaint against the king was this: "He has refused his assent to laws, the most wholesome and necessary for the public good."

Still quoting from Ben Price ...

They were not referring to state laws–there were no "states" yet. They were not referring to national laws–there was no nation yet. What they meant was that the empire was nullifying or "pre-empting" local community laws enacted by direct representatives of the people in the town meetings, county and provincial assemblies, and other community governing bodies throughout the colonies. [emphasis added]

Local self-government has been under attack throughout our country's history. In 1907, professor of Political Science James Allen Smith, published an extraordinary book titled, *The Spirit of American Government.* Here's a short excerpt about local self-government.

These restrictions upon the powers of cities indicate a fear that too much local self-government might jeopardize the interests of the propertied classes. This attitude on the part of those who have framed and interpreted our state constitutions is merely an expression of that distrust of majority rule, which is, as we have seen, the distinguishing feature of the American system of government. It is in the cities that the non-possessing classes are numerically strongest and the inequality in the distribution of wealth most pronounced. This largely explains the reluctance of the state to allow cities a free hand in the management of local affairs. **A municipal government responsive to public opinion might be too much inclined to make the public interests a pretext for disregarding property rights. State control of cities, then, may be regarded as a means of protecting the local minority against the local majority.** Every attempt to reform this system must encounter the opposition of the property-owning class, which is one of the chief reasons why all efforts to establish municipal self-government have thus far largely failed.

Little has changed between 1907, when the professor wrote his book, and the present day. Wherever local communities across this country are trying, within their municipal governments, to exercise the authority they thought they had, they continue to be thwarted. It's not much better at the state level regarding direct democracy either.

Twenty-seven states allow their citizens to exercise direct democracy, where people can gather sufficient signatures to propose specific laws directly to the voters. It is referred to as "initiative and referendum" and it didn't come easily. Massive social movements had to be built across this country in the late 1800s to win this right for We the People. In most states, the state legislatures fought it tooth and nail. They didn't want to have to share governing authority directly with the citizenry.

Yet even in those 27 states with initiative and referendum authority, when citizens organize to improve the health and welfare of their home places, those in positions of power make their work very, very difficult.

We don't live in a society where it is normal for local governments to pass legally-enforceable laws to protect the health and welfare of their communities. In fact, it is illegal. There are two structures of law that make it illegal. One is called Dillon's Rule that I've already discussed. The other structure of law is called state pre-emption. This prohibits local governments from passing laws that ban activities that the state would consider normal and legal: like fracking, factory farming, and clear-cut logging.

There is no right currently in law that protects a community's right of local self-government!

For example, in the state of Oregon where I live, one county after another is currently attempting to pass ballot initiatives that would ban all planting of genetically modified seeds or crops. Our (Democrat Party majority) state legislature came very close early in 2013 to passing a law that would prohibit county governments from banning genetically modified crops. On September 30, 2013, the state legislature is going to make a second attempt to prohibit local decision making authority on this topic. From the state's perspective, GMO agriculture is already regulated, which by their definition means it is considered safe, so it cannot be banned. Therefore, it doesn't matter if a majority of the local community has a different opinion about its safety.

In the state of Georgia, many small rural communities still do not have adequate internet service. In response, local governments had begun to provide municipally-owned internet service. What has been the response from the Georgia legislature? They passed a law that prohibits municipal governments from providing *any* publicly-owned internet service.

In the state of Pennsylvania, many communities have passed bans on corporate fracking and corporate factory farms. In response, the Pennsylvania legislature has passed laws that prohibit local governments from passing such laws. In 2008, then Pennsylvania attorney general and now Governor Thomas Corbett argued before the courts, "There is no inalienable right to local self-government."

Excuse me?!?!

He is actually correct. **There is no right currently in law that protects a community's right of local self-government! The problem is, most Americans think that We the People do possess that right.** We were taught in civics class that we are the sovereign people. So, it makes most of us pretty darn mad when our own elected officials tell us this! Most of us who learn this uncomfortable fact don't tend to take it sitting down. We get active, because we can't believe it could really be true.

A statement like this is especially interesting coming from Pennsylvania, because this state was the only state that produced, in 1776, a truly revolutionary state constitution. It contained a strong declaration of rights. It had a single assembly, chosen by the people and directly responsible to them. All males could vote, including those who didn't own property. Instead of a governor, there was a 12-man executive council directly elected by the people. Wealthy merchants from Philadelphia opposed the constitution, and relentlessly tried to overturn it. In 1790, the state legislature successfully *but illegally* overturned the existing constitution and immediately moved to gut many of its democratic features.

What is most remarkable about governor Corbett's claim is that it's a frontal assault against the Pennsylvania Constitution's own words. Given that Corbett had been the lead attorney in state government before becoming governor, you should have a pretty good idea as to how much he cares about the guarantees in the Pennsylvania State Constitution. Here's Article 1, Section 2, and I quote:

All power is inherent in the people, and all free governments are founded on their authority and instituted for their peace, safety, and happiness. For the advancement of these ends they have at all times an inalienable and indefeasible right to alter, reform, or abolish their government in such manner as they may think proper.

By the way, most state constitutions contain similar language. Since I am speaking today in Iowa, here is the equivalent section of the Iowa State Constitution:

All political power is inherent in the people. Government is instituted for the protection, security, and benefit of the people, and they have the right, at all times, to alter or reform the same, whenever the public good may require it.

And just for good measure, let me also share with you one other state constitution. Here are some brief excerpts from the New Hampshire Constitution's Bill of Rights, which contains some unusual extra language that sets it apart from other state constitutions:

Article 1. All men are born equally free and independent; therefore, all government of right originates from the people, is founded in consent, and instituted for the general good.

Article 7. The people of this state have the sole and exclusive right of governing themselves as a free, sovereign, and independent state;

Article 10. RIGHT OF REVOLUTION. ... Government being instituted for the common benefit, protection, and security, of the whole community, and not for the private interest or emolument of any one man, family, or class of men; therefore, whenever the ends of government are perverted, and public liberty manifestly endangered, and all other means of redress are ineffectual, the people may, and of right ought to reform the old, or establish a new government. The doctrine of non-resistance against arbitrary power, and oppression, is absurd, slavish, and destructive of the good and happiness of mankind.

I'm sharing this text with you simply to remind you that our nation was born of revolution. **Those who came before us rose up against enormous** odds. This language in our state constitutions is one of the only places where you can still catch a glimpse of our early revolutionary history.

Getting back to Pennsylvania, why did Thomas Corbett, now the governor of Pennsylvania, say such an odd thing? Why did he say, "There is no inalienable right to local self-government."?

The fact is that these powerful words in the state constitution are now completely ignored by those in power, in every state in the union, and they will continue to be ignored until We the People remember who We are! In Pennsylvania, the residents have been discovering that they actually don't have very much political power or authority at all. And neither do the people of Georgia or Oregon or any other state for that matter. Their power has been usurped. A whole structure of law has been built over the past 200 years that in effect overrules what the majority wants.

We in the community rights movement have an altogether different idea about what should and should not be allowed. We think that it is what corporations are legally permitted to do that is the real problem here. **When We the People don't challenge the laws that violate our rights, we end up validating those laws with our silence!** We are all about directly confronting unjust laws, just like our ancestors did once upon a time during the American Revolution.

I've described Dillon's Rule, which allows state governments to treat municipal governments and their residents as mere tenants of the state. I've described regulatory law and the regulatory agencies, which tie We the People into knots, making us completely powerless, when we are trying to object to corporate activities that are being planned for our communities. I've described state pre-emption, which prohibits our communities from banning corporate activities that are considered normal and legal under state law.

Corporations now claim a whole set of rights originating in amendments to the Constitution.

The third and final example of a structure of law that neuters our self-governing authority as We the People, which we are also taking on in our work for community rights, is the rise of corporate constitutional so-called "rights" which have overpowered *our* constitutional rights. Allow me to elaborate briefly, and then **I'll share some much more hopeful news** with you about our work and what you can do to get involved to make a difference.

The boards of directors of large corporations have spent most of the past 200 years winning one Supreme Court case after another, embedding into our laws one new corporate constitutional so-called "right" after another. Since 1819, for 194 years and counting, corporations have been expanding *their* legal and political and economic power in our country. The bicentennial of the birth of corporate constitutional so-called "rights" falls in 2019.

Corporations now claim a whole set of rights originating in the amendments to the constitution, all of which are linked to the rights of persons: in other words, corporate personhood rights. These include First Amendment rights to free speech, Fourth Amendment rights against search and seizure, Fifth Amendment rights against takings and due process, Seventh Amendment rights to a jury trial, and Fourteenth Amendment rights to equal protection and due process. If we don't start to pay a lot more attention soon to the constant expansion of corporate "rights," it's just a matter of time before corporate lawyers argue that corporations should be allowed to vote in our elections, or to establish their own militias. We're already heading in that direction.

Here's a test question for you:

What can you do when a corporation violates your free speech rights, or your property rights, or your privacy rights?

The answer might surprise you! There's actually *nothing* you can do, at least within conventional law! You know why? Because the Bill of Rights only protects you when the *government* violates your rights. It offers you absolutely no protection when a corporation violates your rights. Given that corporations have become the dominant institution of our society and our world, that's a pretty darn scary situation.

In addition, corporations claim rights directly from the constitution itself. The U.S. Supreme Court has "found" corporate rights in the Commerce Clause, the Contracts Clause, and the Diversity Clause. I say that the court has "found" corporate rights in those sections of the constitution, because the word "corporation" doesn't exist anywhere in the constitution. This is an outstanding example of what we call judge-made law, and **judges are not supposed to make law.**

Here's a recent example of corporate "rights" overpowering our rights here in Iowa. The state of Iowa has a law, written in 1975, that is designed to keep large corporate meat packers from controlling livestock farming, a practice known as vertical integration. The law was originally written "in order to preserve free and private enterprise, prevent monopoly, and protect consumers."

Unfortunately, Iowa's law has run afoul of corporate constitutional "rights" repeatedly and is no longer being enforced for this reason. Texas Farm Corporation, a Texas-based hog company, was the latest company to sue the state in April, 2013. Previously, Iowa has been sued by Smithfield Foods, Cargill, Hormel Foods, Tyson Fresh Meats, and other meat companies. What was the legal claim that all of these corporations used against the state? They all alleged that the state's law violated the Commerce Clause of the U.S. Constitution. The Clause has been interpreted by the courts to mean that states may not pass laws that discriminate against out-of-state businesses in favor of those in the state. In response to each of these cases, the state has agreed to not enforce its own law! This is what happens when We the People allow corporations to claim constitutional "rights." It's not a pretty picture.

What do you say we decide here and now that we will declare 2019, which is the bicentennial of corporate "rights," as the year that corporate "rights" are ended in this country. Enough is enough! What do you say? Are you with me?

We have all been trained to see large corporations as these tremendously powerful forces that can push us aside and do whatever they want.

Let's not forget: a corporation is just *property*, shares of which are owned by human beings. It is referred to in the law as a legal fiction, because it doesn't actually exist in the material world. It is merely a business structure. **Giving rights to a corporation is like giving rights to the number six. It's absurd! We don't give free speech rights to houses. We don't give property rights to chairs.** We don't because it's silly. Yet we have allowed our courts to give all sorts of constitutional "rights" to business structures called corporations.

But that's not all. It gets more absurd. Our corporate accountability movements and corporate social responsibility movements then attempt to hold the corporate "it" accountable, which is ridiculous if you really think about it.

When your toaster stops working, do you try to hold it accountable? Do you march up and down in front of it, shouting slogans at it? Do you negotiate with it? Do you plead with it? No, of course not. It's simply a tool; it toasts your bread. When it stops working, you understand that it is you who needs to be responsible for fixing it or replacing it. **Corporations are supposed to be our tools, the tools of a sovereign people.** When they stop doing the job they were designed to do, it is we who are responsible for setting things right. It is we who must hold their *directors* accountable. Believe it or not, that's how it once was after the American Revolution, when it was understood by both politicians and the general public that a corporation was a legally subordinate entity that existed to serve the public good and to cause no harm.

For years I have said that we need to de-personify the corporate "it" and personify the actual decision-makers hiding behind the corporate veil.

Think about the *Wizard of Oz* with me for a moment. We see an image of the great Oz on a projection screen. His voice bellows. Dorothy and her friends tremble with fear in front of his image. Toto, the little dog, runs to a curtain on the side of the room and pulls it open to expose a small man pulling levers and speaking into a microphone. This is actually a perfect symbol of what I'm describing.

We have all been trained to see large corporations as these tremendously powerful forces that can push us aside and do whatever they want to do in our communities. **As long as we believe that they are this powerful, then in fact they ARE this powerful. But in reality, they are merely illusions of power.** Like the great Oz, they don't exist in reality at all. They are merely business structures, with decision makers hiding behind curtains, making demands upon us. So, why do we act so powerless in their presence?

Imagine if we responded, not to their image on the screen, but instead to the actual human beings who are hiding from us, the ones who are pulling the levers. It is they whom we must hold personally accountable when the corporate "it" causes serious harms to our communities, because they are the ones who make the actual decisions that cause the actual harms in the places where we live.

Did you know that it wasn't until 1919 that corporations were required to maximize returns to their shareholders? That was just another court decision. Before then, corporate directors had much more freedom to decide what to do with the profits they made.

Even liability protections are something new. After the American Revolution, corporate directors and shareholders were held personally liable for all harms and debts caused by the corporation.

So, you see, we can't even assume that we know what a corporation is, because it is defined by those in state government who bring corporations into existence in the first place. Historically, corporations were created one at a time by state legislatures, and their directors and stockholders had to abide by a whole litany of requirements and prohibitions.

Imagine what would have happened, after the British Petroleum Corporation oil spill in the Gulf of Mexico, if our nation's early corporate chartering laws were still in place. I can tell you what would have happened. BP's directors would have never decided to drill in such deep water in the first place, nor would the stockholders have allowed such risky corporate behavior, because all of these players would have known that they could end up in jail if something had gone wrong. Or their personal assets could have been seized. Or the corporation itself could have been dissolved through a charter revocation action by the government. Instead, because corporations are now packed to the gills with constitutional so-called "rights," all we can do is beg and plead with their liability-protected directors to cause a little less harm the next time. That's no way to run a society that is supposed to be based on a revolutionary truth, that all power is inherent in The People. We have drifted a long way from that reality.

> *We don't have a left wing versus right wing problem in this country. We have a top 1% versus the bottom 99% problem.*

That is why I said earlier that we must learn to de-personify the corporate "it" and personify the actual decision-makers hiding behind the corporate veil. For when we do this, we start to find it strange that a corporate "it" should have more rights than We do. We start to question the validity of legal structures that have been placed as barriers in front of us, legal structures like corporate constitutional so-called "rights," and state pre-emption laws that prohibit us from protecting our own communities from harm, and

Dillon's Rule, that treats We the People as children, and regulatory laws that are designed to ignore our opposition to destructive corporate activities.

It's not going to be enough if we simply work harder to elect good people to government. The problem is much more serious than that. We need to stop focusing on candidates and instead focus on the actual structures of law that create this reality in the first place. I am convinced that the local democracy work that is already happening in 160 communities in nine states, including Winneshiek County, Iowa, is the most powerful response that I personally have ever seen, in more than 37 years as a grassroots community organizer.

As James Madison said so clearly, the primary purpose of government is to serve the elite. The Occupy movement understood this truth. I think the Tea Party also understands this truth. We don't have a left wing versus rightwing problem in this country. We have a top 1% versus the bottom 99% problem. Our system of government is designed to benefit a very small number of us. Therefore, in order to tackle the problem, we need to tackle the design of the system of laws that govern us.

Again, quoting Ben Price:

> State laws that deny the authority of community governments to protect their health, safety, welfare, and quality of life violate fundamental rights. State laws that exempt agribusiness, energy, waste hauling, water wholesalers, and other corporations from being governed locally, place the privileges of wealth and property over the democratic rights of citizens to determine the future of their own communities. Local officials regularly confess to their constituents that they wish they could do more, but their "hands are tied" by state pre-emptive law. These officials are told that if they honor their oaths to protect the health, safety, and welfare of the community, they will be breaking state law.

In Winneshiek County, in the northeast corner of Iowa, local elected officials who were simply trying to do the job they were elected to do, have experienced exactly the same sort of push-back from corporations and state government as have their counterparts in other states.

Here are some examples:

- WalMart Corporation wanted to build on a flood plain, which violated local laws. The local government was pressured to retrospectively change their laws, to assist the corporation's law-breaking activity.

- A waste management corporation wanted to buy the local landfill and turn it into a waste incinerator. In order to stop this corporate plan, the local government had no choice but to buy it themselves.

- A corporate property owner, Riverbend Land Development Corporation, wanted to put in a subdivision below an eagle's nest in a vulnerable ecosystem. Ultimately the National Heritage Foundation had to buy the land, simply to protect the area.

- A number of historic local buildings have been bulldozed, against the wishes of many local residents, and in spite of their being listed on the National Register of Historic Places.

- It is a constant struggle to get pesticide spraying stopped around local schools, hospitals, and wellheads.

- And most recently, the Winneshiek County Board of Supervisors voted unanimously to deny the necessary permit to the latest factory farm application from Millennium Agriculture Corporation. The Department of Natural Resources then ignored the vote of the local elected officials and approved the permit (which is what agencies like this usually do) so it is now being appealed to the Environmental Protection Commission, which is also likely to approve the permit. This is how the system works in conventional law! This is how the system is designed to operate. Why? Because the Board of Supervisors' decision violates the corporation's so-called "rights" as well as violating state pre-emption and Dillon's Rule.

Is this really the kind of powerlessness that we wish on our local elected officials, who have given oaths to protect the health, safety, and welfare of their community? I don't think so!

These are just a few examples of what happens on the ground, in every local community in this country, when corporations have more rights than we do, and when our state government is allowed to utterly ignore the will of the local residents.

It is time to become a lot less obedient to the laws that violate our rights. It is time to refamiliarize ourselves with our own revolutionary history. Because when we do, we are going to realize that our current situation is eerily similar to that of the early colonists preparing themselves for revolution against the king. It took them decades to shift from begging the king to provide more liberty, to declaring that their patience had worn thin and beginning to exercise their inherent right to govern themselves. To exercise that right required massive acts of civil disobedience.

What will it take for We the People of every town and city across this country to reach the point where we declare that our patience has worn thin also? That it's time to exercise our inherent right to govern ourselves? What will it take? How many violations of our rights will it take for us to stand together as community majorities and say boldly to all who wish to hear us: "No more!"

Before I'm completely out of time tonight, I really want to tell you about some extraordinary developments that are taking place across the country. For the past 13 years, in 160 communities in nine states, people have been rising up and doing something that hasn't really taken place in this country since the Abolitionist and Suffragist movements of the 1800s.

We call ourselves the community rights movement, and like the early colonists in the American Revolution, we are refusing to abide by unjust laws. We are passing local laws that very publicly and directly confront corporate constitutional "rights" and state government authority to overrule local decision making. One of my mentors in this work, Thomas Linzey, refers to this local law-making as "collective acts of municipal civil disobedience." Some people would say that our local laws are illegal. We prefer to say that they are not legal *yet*. Because, like the Suffragists and Abolitionists who came before us, sometimes unjust laws have to be violated over and over and over before new laws can take their place.

One of the seminal moments early on in the Civil Rights movement in the South was when four young adults sat down together at a lunch counter and refused to move. They had no idea whether their actions would be noticed or not outside of their own community. No one could have predicted that within weeks of their action, hundreds of lunch counter sit-ins would be happening across the southern states. That small action of four young people caused a cultural eruption that lit up the whole country. What will be our lunch counter moment? Obviously, I can't answer that question but I have a pretty good idea that the community rights movement will soon reach deep into enough communities and that we too are going to see a cultural eruption that will be impossible to stop. Because people across this beautiful country, across political ideologies, are growing sick and tired of the rights of We the People being trampled on.

I am one of the lead organizers of this work in the Pacific Northwest and am increasingly being invited to travel across the country to assist communities that are considering joining us.

The movement began in the year 2000, when about 20 conservative rural farming communities across Pennsylvania passed laws that banned non-family-owned corporations from engaging in farming or owning farmland. These farm communities had learned that this was possible after discovering that nine states had previously passed anti-corporate farming laws, beginning in the early 1900s. Other rural Pennsylvania communities then followed suit, banning corporations from dumping urban sewage sludge on their farmland. It then spread to other states.

Communities in Maine and New Hampshire banned corporations from setting up water bottling facilities. The city of Pittsburgh banned fracking by a vote of seven to zero in its city council just a few years later when it passed a Right to Water ordinance. Many other communities followed their lead. Most recently, the voters in State College, Pennsylvania, banned any further so-called "natural" gas pipelines from being placed under their town, with a whopping 72% majority. Mora County, New Mexico, just became the first county in the country this year to ban all oil drilling, fracking, and other hydrocarbon removal. Four towns in New Hampshire voted overwhelmingly last year in their annual Town Meetings to protect the residents' Right to a Sustainable Energy Future by banning energy transmission lines that are intended to pass through their towns.

Where I live in Oregon, five counties are actively engaged in community rights local law-making campaigns. Two rural counties are working hard to pass ordinances that would protect their Right to a Local Food System and would ban all GMO agriculture. Another county is hoping to pass an ordinance that would protect their Right to a Sustainable Economy and would ban all raw log exports from their port town. In the city of Portland, where I live, we are in the early stages of figuring out how we might pass a local law or charter amendment that would enshrine for all residents the Right to Live in an Economically and Ecologically Sustainable City. (See

"A Community Bill of Rights for Portland, Oregon ... or Any Community!" on page 140.)

All of our current ordinances also include a recognition that our local ecosystems have a locally-enforceable right to exist, flourish, and evolve. And, as I described earlier in my talk, our ordinances refuse to recognize state pre-emption or Dillon's Rule, when these state laws violate our inherent right of local self-governance. They nullify corporate constitutional so-called "rights" within the boundaries of our communities.

We invite you to join us in this rapidly growing network of 160 communities in nine states. Earlier this year, people in Allamakee and Winneshiek counties were introduced to our work when I came to town. Four months ago, the Community Rights Alliance of Winneshiek County was formed with the goal of using the community rights strategy to pass a local ordinance that would ban the very destructive process of frac sand mining here in this beautiful place. I applaud those of you who are already active in this local campaign and encourage the rest of you to jump on board.

Can I ask the members of the Community Rights Alliance of Winneshiek County to stand for a moment so that you can see who's already doing this work here? Please consider joining them!

Frac sand mining can be stopped here before it starts, but it's going to take a courageous effort on the part of your local elected officials to pass a rights-based local law to stop it. You are simply not going to be able to stop frac sand mining here using a conventional regulatory approach (and we've got 40 years of evidence to prove it) whereas 160 communities in nine states have already stopped destructive corporate activities using rights-based local law-making.

Our nation and our world are in crisis. Our ecological systems are collapsing. Our economy increasingly resembles a house of cards. Working people are getting squeezed more and more each year. All of these crises can be addressed in powerful new ways if we start to exercise our inherent right of local self-governance.

To take this work one step further, we are also in the early stages of creating state-wide community rights networks, which will focus their energies on taking back our state laws and state constitutions so that they can no longer be used to violate our rights as We the People. Ultimately, our state networks will be forming a national community rights network, because we also have to take back our federal laws and constitution, as they are currently elevating corporate constitutional "rights" over *our* rights, and property rights over everyone's right to live in safe and healthy communities. And that is simply not acceptable.

It doesn't matter whether you're a Republican or a Democrat, a Libertarian, or a Green. We need all hands on deck! **This time, it's not the king who is threatening us. It's the very structures of law that are causing so much harm in our communities.** In response, we must figure out how to work together, and build majority support to protect our communities. All of us desire to live in a locality and a country where our inherent right to govern ourselves is respected by all of our elected officials, and where our corporate institutions are not constantly violating our rights.

> *It doesn't matter whether you're a Republican*
> *or a Democrat, a Libertarian, or a Green.*
> *We need all hands on deck!*

Before I conclude my talk, I'd like to share an amazing opinion piece that I received this week, written by Gail Darrell and other members of the New Hampshire Community Rights Network. I had mentioned previously that four New Hampshire communities had passed ordinances defending the right to a sustainable energy future and banning long-distance transmission lines through their communities from Canada. This is from one of those communities.

The land and the reputation that we've inherited from our ancestors have been built from strong stock. Whether we've lived close to the land here for generations or have come "from away" to escape the industrialization of our former homes, we have learned how to adapt to a climate that changes practically every ten minutes. The one thing that will never change is our love for the mountains, rivers, streams, and rural communities that is more than a backdrop picture for our lives.

We've been sending a strong message to Hydro-Quebec, Northern Pass and the corporate partnership built on the promise of more, for over three years. We understand that it takes people seven times before they can hear and internalize new material. **We wonder if there is a learning impairment involved that prevents the corporate ownership of one of the** most destructive hydroelectric projects on the planet from comprehending the meaning of "no," or the message of, "not now, not ever."

If New Hampshire needs more energy, we should create state-wide initiatives to support and allow local communities to replace fossil fuel consumption with sustainable energy solutions that reflect our way of life. We never asked for, nor do we require, any foreign or corporate entity to create and impose policies on our people without our consent.

It's time to stand up for our communities and our values. To not back down, never apologize and never compromise on rights. Government of right originates in the people and operates by consent. The State operates at the peoples' behest, not the other way around. This is not an argument about electricity; it's an argument about rights. No permit for the project, no compromise on rights and no Northern Pass. Not in my backyard, not in anyone's backyard. Not now, not ever.

I urge you to get involved in your community. Please contact me, Paul Cienfuegos, and my partners at Community Rights US, to find out how we can assist you and your community. Thank you so very much!

All Power is Inherent
in the People ...
But Only if We *Act*
As if We Believe It

*I wrote the following as a commentary/podcast for the KBOO Evening News
in Portland, Oregon on January 6, 2015.*

This is my first commentary of the 2015 new year. I thought I would begin by talking a bit about what democracy is. It's a word that is incredibly overused in this country. We are told by our corporate media that our government is exporting democracy to other countries, which usually translates as forcing corporate capitalism on other sovereign nations. In fact, **it has become normal for our corporate media and government to use the words democracy and capitalism interchangeably,** which just blows my mind.

This nation was founded in revolution. Virtually all of the revolutionary language that originated at that time has been stripped from our laws and constitutional structures. There are a few exceptions. One of these exceptions is the opening paragraph of each of our state constitutions. Very few Americans know anything about that paragraph, and that's a real shame.

Our Oregon State Constitution was approved by a vote of the people in 1857. Here's how it starts:

> **Natural rights inherent in people.** We declare that all men,
> when they form a social compact are equal in right: that all
> power is inherent in the people, and all free governments are
> founded on their authority, and instituted for their peace,
> safety, and happiness; and they have at all times a right to alter,

reform, or abolish the government in such manner as they may think proper.

Them's fightin' words!

What would change in our country if We the People started acting again as if we believed those words to be true, that all power is inherent in the people, that all free governments are founded on *our authority*, and that we have, at all times, a right to alter, reform, or abolish our government when we deem it necessary?

Those words pretty much sum up what real democracy would look like and feel like. The word democracy itself has a very powerful definition. It comes from two Latin words, *demos* and *cratia*, which literally means *rule by the people*, and, if you think about it, matches the opening paragraph of our state constitution.

Now I want to ask you a question: **When is the last time you reflected on what it might look like if you yourself participated in your community, not as a single-issue activist and not as a consumer who votes with your dollars, but as a member of the collective body known as We the People, who together have the authority to govern ourselves?**

Democracy: rule by the people. Most Americans have become so profoundly cynical about our country's so-called democracy that they have almost entirely tuned out and turned off. I don't call this apathy. In fact, I think it's a quite rational response to a system that was in fact designed to appear as if it was a functioning democratic republic, when it was actually designed to serve the wealthy elite, which it does quite well.

Real democracy, unlike the "democracy theme park" (coined by Jane Anne Morris) we now inhabit, would engage all of us. We would know it was the real thing because of how we would feel participating in it. **My work in the community rights movement is all about engaging the citizenry to start acting again as if we really do have the authority to govern ourselves, because in fact we do, if we think and act like we do.** To get there requires real effort, not just pushing keys on our keyboard to support the latest online petition to some power-holder somewhere.

Douglas Lummis, author of the amazing book, *Radical Democracy*, describes real democracy as a state of being, the art of the possible, a state of public hope, a performance art. He says that real democracy is a very scale-sensitive process, very place-oriented. It thrives where people are close to each other and living in place. It is a belief in ourselves, he says.

Our nation's so-called founding fathers were terrified of real democracy. They placed trust in autonomy and in individual rights, not in connection or collective wisdom. They sought stability and security through the ownership of property, rather than through people's relationship with each other. They valued liberty but linked it to property rather than to relationship. **Freedom was defined as the freedom to do what you want with what you own.** So, it is no wonder that we ended up in the mess we are in today.

> *Our nation's so-called founding fathers were*
> *terrified of real democracy.*

How do we dig ourselves out of this deep hole? By moving away from this rugged individualist version of liberty and moving towards collective action that is place-based and scale-sensitive. Imagine the residents of each city and town across this huge country choosing to organize themselves in this way. Imagine what might naturally occur in every city and town if the people took the language of their state constitutions to heart, and started to act as if they actually believed it to be true: that all power *is* inherent in the people, that all free governments *are* founded on our authority, and that we have at all times a *right* to alter, reform or abolish our government when we deem it necessary.

This is *not* Marxism or communism or socialism. This is *our own revolutionary history*, and it's time we again started acting as We the People.

How would we arrange ourselves? What kinds of institutions and strategies would yield the goals we are striving for? What skills would we need to learn in order to practice the arts of democracy? We have real work to do.

Got Property Rights?
You Have the Right
to Destroy Planet Earth!

I wrote this as a commentary/podcast for the KBOO Evening News in Portland, Oregon on August 25, 2015.

After the American Revolution, our so-called "founding fathers" drafted a constitution that was intended to last for a very long time. They titled it The Articles of Confederation and Perpetual Union. In many ways it was a truly revolutionary document. Primary decision-making authority was held individually by 13 sovereign states, in a confederated structure with some similarities to the current European Union. At the federal level, there was no executive branch. There was no judicial branch.

For many of the wealthy elite, our first constitution was an unacceptable document, as it prioritized decentralized decision making at the state and local level, which was, by definition, more participatory. The elite were more interested in creating an empire in the new world. This required a fundamental shift towards a federal system of governance, with states playing second fiddle. It took only one decade for this elite to orchestrate what some refer to as a political coup.

Rights for The People were added later,
as amendments to our second constitution,
to quiet the rabble with nice sounding phrases.

Representatives from all 13 states were supposed to meet in a "grand convention" in Philadelphia to amend the existing constitution, but instead, they tossed it out entirely and wrote a second constitution from scratch. When it was time to ask the states to ratify this new constitution, the general response was outrage, as it said virtually nothing about the rights of people. In fact, the new constitution was primarily about property and commerce. The ruling elite now had what they wanted: a strong federal system of governance, and a weak state and local system of governance. **Now, the elite could start mobilizing to build what became the greatest empire in the history of the world.**

Yes, there was ultimately a set of rights established for The People, but only as a side agreement. Rights for The People were added later, as amendments to our second constitution, to quiet the rabble with nice sounding phrases that supposedly protected their rights, but only around the edges. The elite had won. The country was now constitutionally defined as one in which those with property had the rights that really mattered, and where commerce and trade trumped all other societal activities.

Today in 2015, we inhabit a nation where property rights, commerce, and trade are still considered the holy grail. But most of us have forgotten, or never knew, how we arrived at this situation. **Since the ratification of our second U.S. Constitution, property rights have trumped the rights of the people.** It's really that simple. It's really that stark. Property rights are now embedded in how we think about our country. Like fish in water, we assume the way we live is background normal. I could offer you a very long list of examples. Here are just three.

- If we live in a house or apartment as renters, we have very few rights, whereas our landlord, be they human or corporate, have all the rights that matter, which means we can be evicted on the slimmest of excuses. Can we evict our landlord? Of course not. What a silly idea!

- If we work for wages, we have very few rights, whereas our employer, be they human or corporate, have all the rights that matter. Most of us are "at will" employees, which means we can be fired for no reason at all. Can we fire our boss? Of course not. What a silly idea!

- If we stand at a major business intersection in most cities and towns, what we are witnessing with our own eyes and ears is a breath-taking example of the propertied class making virtually all of the land use decisions that matter. Will the scale of buildings be in relationship to the size of our human bodies, or will they make us look like ants? Will the businesses be locally owned? Will they be cooperatively managed by their employees? Will they have the same corporate logos and product offerings as most of the other business intersections across the landscape? Will the roads favor pedestrians and bicyclists, or will they favor cars and trucks? Will the original landscape of forest, meadow, creek, and cliff still be visible, or will it have been erased entirely many decades ago? All of these are absolutely critical decisions that can make or break a sense of community, equity and sustainability. Yet most of these decisions were made by those who once owned the properties that surround you. You are literally surrounded by property rights. Your community is drowning in property rights.

If you own property, there are three things that you are legally entitled to do with that property. First, you have the constitutional right to use that property however you wish. Second, you have the right to exclude others from using that property. And third, you have the right to destroy whatever is alive on that property. You can fill in your wetland. You can clear-cut your forest. You can re-contour your landscape. You can poison your wildlife. You can pave your meadow. Yes, there are some legal limits, but you have the constitutional right to sue for a taking of your property if the rules are not to your liking, and to be reimbursed, at taxpayer expense, for your loss of future profits. (When it's corporations that own property, and thus can exercise their so-called property "rights," look out!)

Now, let's extend this extraordinary reality to a much larger scale. The most valuable private property that exists today in the U.S. is the business corporation itself. Our largest corporations have economies larger than major nation states. Business corporations are themselves considered private property, and those who run these corporations have the legal and constitutional authority to exercise their corporate property "rights." These corporate property "rights" exist because the Supreme Court says they exist. End of story! A corporation that is itself private property has been granted constitutional "rights." Oh my!

If your community is filled with chain stores, it is because the owners of those stores were (and still are) exercising their corporate property "rights," which trump the rights of the citizens of that place. **If your rural community was once surrounded by healthy forests and streams, which are now gone, it's because the owners or leasers of those forests were (and still are) exercising their corporate property "rights," which trump the rights of the residents of your community.** I could give example after example.

As you look around you, where you live, how many of the land use decisions in that place are made publicly and transparently by those who live there? How many are made by those who own the property? How much longer can we survive on this planetary orb floating in deep space, when virtually every decision that matters to us is being made without our involvement? What is it going to take for We the People to say, "Enough already!" and to institute truly democratic decision-making processes in our communities?

The Right of Local
Self-Government:
This is What Democracy
Actually Looks Like

*I wrote this as a commentary/podcast for the KBOO Evening News
in Portland, Oregon on January 19, 2016.*

I was one of the lucky ones who got to spend an entire week in the streets and at the teach-ins in downtown Seattle, beginning on November 30, 1999, when the World Trade Organization made the fateful mistake of bringing their international trade negotiations conference to the Pacific Northwest's largest city. **Over several extraordinary days, at least 60,000 citizens came together from across the world and successfully shut down the WTO's obscene gathering of corporate and government leaders who were there to carve up the planet for profit.** This scale of public outrage had never been seen before at a global trade negotiation, and it rocked the corporate board-rooms.

Yet there was still something that wasn't quite right about our big success. There we were, day after day, marching through downtown Seattle, creating traffic chaos, and chanting, "This is what democracy looks like; this is what democracy looks like." And all the time, I kept thinking to myself, "Actually, this is not at all what real democracy looks like." **In an authentic and well-functioning democratic society, the public would not have to march down the middle of a street to get its own government to pay attention.** We would not have to put our bodies on the line, risking arrest, to shut down a corporate trade treaty organization. We the People would be the ones sitting around the table, deciding what sort of trade was ecologically and economically sustainable, and therefore allowed to proceed. But that felt more like a dream than anything that could be achieved anytime soon.

So, as we marched, I found myself chanting a subtly different refrain, "This is *not* what democracy looks like; this is *not* what democracy looks like." Amusingly, people who were marching beside me would hear my words, and would laugh, and then they too would start to chant, "This is *not* what democracy looks like." At least we felt a little bit powerful, because we were 60,000 strong, We the People of Planet Earth. Yes, I was tear gassed that week more times than I can remember. **Yes, I saw levels of police violence against nonviolent demonstrators that made my blood boil. But even this was a good thing for this privileged white boy to experience with my own eyes.**

Since 1999, I have done a lot of thinking about what genuine democracy might look like, and how we might get there in these disUnited States of America. Right around that same time, I got involved in what has come to be known as the community rights movement. I was one of the movement's earliest organizers and workshop leaders, which is the work I still do today. We have now helped about 200 communities in nine states to reclaim the self-governing authority that was stolen from communities, just one decade after the Declaration of Independence was written, when James Madison and George Washington and others organized a political coup in this country. That coup tossed out our founding constitution which was titled The Articles of Confederation and Perpetual Union, a constitution that had recognized that local communities had self-governing authority. The history of this brief period has been mostly forgotten until recently. Here's a little nibble of that history, excerpted from a wonderful new booklet titled, *The People's Right of Local Community Self-Government*. All text in quotes is from the booklet.

> The colonists' struggle with British rule illustrates how community self-government took shape as the foundation of the American system of constitutional law. The colonists' efforts culminated in the *Declaration of Independence*, which codified the principles of local self-government that had been forged by American settlements since the 1600s. [In fact,] the concept of community self-government in America dates back

to the *Mayflower Compact,* adopted in 1620, [which] was the first constitution of its kind to be written by the American colonists. In one paragraph, [it] dismantled the old system of government, based on royal authority, and forged a new one based purely on the political sovereignty of the people themselves.

> *It is the people who give the state the authority to govern and not the other way around.*

This laser focus on the right of local self-government continued throughout the 1700s and into the founding of states with their own constitutions. For example, in Pennsylvania's Declaration of Rights, incorporated in the Pennsylvania Constitution of 1776, the people declare,

> That government is, or ought to be, instituted for the common benefit, protection and security of the people, nation, or community; and not for the particular emolument or advantage of any single man, family, or set of men, who are a part only of that community; and that the community hath an indubitable, unalienable and indefeasible right to reform, alter, or abolish government in such manner as shall be by that community judged most conducive to the public weal.

> The Pennsylvania Constitution [also] made clear that the people's right of self-government could not be overridden by other levels of government. [That in fact] the people's inherent inalienable rights are forever superior to the state government [and] not subject to control by the state government.

> The right of local, community self-government ... is also protected by the Ninth Amendment of the Bill of Rights. [Although all of this is historical fact,] community law-making ... has generated mostly critical, occasionally derisive treatment from legislators, jurists, and commentators.

Legal doctrines have been concocted to severely restrict local power, such as corporate constitutional so-called "rights," Dillon's Rule, and state pre-emption.

Yet, believe it or not, "it is the people who give the state the authority to govern and not the other way around." This deeper truth is what energizes the community rights movement, now active in about 15 states, as we work to bring this early American history back to life and help citizens to realize that our right of community self-government is not some pie in the sky notion, but something grounded directly in the American Revolution. We believe that if a local community majority cannot exercise its authority to protect its own health and welfare, then we cannot honestly claim that we live in a democratic society. Therefore, our movement is attempting to reawaken The People to claim our rightful place at the center of decision making. I invite you to join us where you live!

Common Sense Rules
for Controlling Corporations

This is a reproduction of a two-page educational flyer distributed by Community Rights US.

Are you concerned about the rapid growth of corporate power in your community and beyond? So are we! Did you know there's actually something we can do to reverse this trend?

Here are some common sense rules that would make a huge difference in shifting the balance of power from corporations to We the People.

✔ No corporation shall be allowed to participate in any way in the political process, at any level of government. No corporate financing of candidates or ballot initiatives. No corporate lobbying of elected or appointed government officials, or of those running for office at any level of government. No political advertising by corporations.

✔ Directors and stockholders of corporations shall be held personally and individually liable for all harms and debts caused during the time such persons directed or held stock in that corporation.

✔ No corporation shall be allowed to merge with another corporation, to own shares in another corporation, or to be purchased by another corporation.

✔ No corporation shall be allowed to donate money or services to any civic or charitable organizations. We the People cannot afford to become financially dependent on the "generosity" of large corporations as we are then forced to remain silent when those very corporations commit serious harms or crimes.

✔ Corporate shareholders shall have the right to remove directors at will.

I can already hear you shaking your head, having decided that these rules are pie in the sky and could NEVER become law in this country!

Are you ready to be shocked? Are you sitting down?

Every single rule listed above was the law of the land in these United States of America after the American Revolution. These were all state laws, but they were mostly repealed as a direct result of hundreds of Supreme Court decisions beginning in 1819, which enshrined more and more constitutional so-called "rights" for corporations, in effect overruling the rights that We the People assumed were about us!

If you didn't already know this history, perhaps you should ask yourself WHY you didn't **know this. Perhaps the powers that be would much rather you not know your own history? Because if you knew this history, you would be MUCH more likely to insist that these common sense laws be reinstituted. Right?**

But there's more! Here are additional state laws that we've lost.

✔ All corporations, be they owned or controlled by U.S. citizens or foreigners, shall be chartered (i.e. brought into legal existence) by a state government, to fulfill one specific purpose, to serve the common good, and to cause no harm. Corporate charters must be renewed every ten to forty years, depending on the nature of the business. Bank charters shall be renewed every three to ten years.

✔ State legislatures shall have the authority to amend or revoke a corporate charter at any time by majority vote. Unless a state legislature renews an expiring charter, the corporation will be dissolved and its assets divided among the stockholders.

✔ Corporate financial and other records shall be fully accessible to all state legislators, and other state elected officials.

✔ Corporations shall not be allowed to own land, except when explicitly allowed to do so in order to fulfill the purpose of their charter. Corporations which have been granted the privilege of land ownership are prohibited from selling or speculating on their land. Corporate ownership of land comes to an end when the corporation's charter expires or is revoked.

✔ The power of large corporate shareholders shall be limited by scaled voting, so that large and small investors have equal voting rights.

✔ The penalty for abuse or misuse of the charter, and/or for any violations of the above rules, is revocation of the charter, and the dissolution of the corporation.

✔ Corporate acts not authorized by law are *ultra vires* (or "beyond the authority") of corporations, and are therefore grounds for charter revocation.

Did you know any of this history? Are you stunned? Does this information make you feel more hopeful about the possibility for real change? Do you want to know more?

There is a growing movement in this country intent on nothing less than taking back our country from large out-of-control corporations and the 1% who run them. We call ourselves the community rights movement. Because we've lost a LOT of legal (and cultural) ground over these past two centuries, we're starting from the ground up, reigning in corporate so-called "rights" one town, city, and county at a time until we've gained enough traction to reclaim our state and federal laws. Our history shows that this is indeed possible!

More than 200 communities in 12 states have already passed locally enforceable community rights laws banning all sorts of harmful corporate activities, exercising our inherent right of local self-government, and stripping corporations of so-called "rights."

Would you like to know more?

Please visit www.CommunityRights.US to learn about the local laws we've been passing for more than two decades. You can sign up for our newsletter there, or make a donation, or volunteer, or sign up for a workshop. We look forward to hearing from you!

The preceding document is one of Community Rights US' educational pieces. Let's take this one step further, shall we?

Imagine how quickly and dramatically our society would improve if these sets of laws were reinstated today. But why should we stop there? These rules were written in the 1800s! We live in an entirely different world now. Here are some of my ideas for additional rules that corporations could be required to follow:

- Single-use packaging of any kind shall be prohibited, unless it can be proven to be biodegradable.

- The maximum ratio between compensation of the highest and lowest paid employee shall not exceed 5:1.

- Corporations shall not do business under pseudonyms or alternative names.

- All stockholders shall have one vote each regardless of share ownership.

- A 60% state-wide referendum vote shall be required to renew a corporate charter.

- Native American treaty-protected rights to access local lands and waters shall be recognized, honored and enforced.

- Corporations shall pay all externalized social and environmental costs associated with their operations.

- Corporations shall be prohibited from employing replacement workers during strikes.

- The fundamental constitutional Bill of Rights protections (free speech, assembly, privacy, etc.) of all corporate employees while they are at work shall be fully protected and enforced.

- Corporations shall not be permitted to take tax deductions for lawyers' fees, advertising or fines.

- Production, investment and distribution decisions shall be made by citizens and implemented by corporations, not the other way around.

- Corporations shall be prohibited from financing or designing any scientific research programs.

- Whenever corporate directors refuse to cooperate with the community's objectives, eminent domain laws shall be used to acquire corporate property and place it under local public control.

- Items produced in foreign sweatshops shall be banned from sale in local shops.

- Local grocery stores shall reserve a growing percentage of shelf space for products grown or produced within 500 miles, phased in over five to ten years.

- Corporations shall be required to meet strict renewable energy and waste stream standards.

- Local natural areas shall have enforceable rights to exist, flourish and evolve.

- Democratic planning and decision-making authority shall be implemented at the neighborhood level.

The possibilities are endless! You can view the list of additional climate-protection-related local ordinance ideas at www.CommunityRights.US/Book.

Taking Our Language Back
from Corporate Culture

I wrote this originally in 2001 for the Reclaim Democracy group's newsletter which chose not to use it. Years later, I published it on my blog in January 2010 and I continue to update it. Unfortunately, it is as relevant today as it was way back in 2001.

The founding fathers of our nation never intended for the institution called "corporation" to have any authority over We the People at all. The word "corporation" appears nowhere in any of the nation's founding documents. Yet today, most Americans accept that the corporate "it" has enormous power and authority to shape our lives, and we assume that it always did.

Today, we can barely tell the difference between the rights of an actual person and the supposed rights of a corporate "it," as both are now protected by many of the amendments in the Bill of Rights. (The Supreme Court granted personhood to the corporation in 1886.) Both we and our corporate creations are guaranteed free speech and property protections, are protected against unreasonable search and seizure, and cannot be hindered in our writing of contracts with each other.

Of course, the problem with this is that corporate "persons" aren't persons at all. They're really just property, owned and managed by investors, stockholders and directors, with the actual "workers" somehow mysteriously left out of the decision-making loop, even though without them, the corporation would be hollow, worthless, and meaningless. **In effect, our judges have given constitutional rights to property** which, I'm sure you'll agree, is pretty silly.

Imagine how different society might look if we, the *real* people (what I like to call "people with skin"), stopped playing this shell game, and started treating corporations like the legal fictions they really are: with no legitimate rights and with no legitimate authority over us, as they once were prior to the late 1800s. Mere tools of a sovereign people, like a toaster or a toilet. You don't boycott or plead with or punish or sue or negotiate with your toilet when it refuses to do its job. Why should we treat *our subordinate corporate creations* any differently?

With that idea in mind, let's explore how our language creates reality. It is one of our most potent ways of making sense of our world. And when we use the *language* of corporate personhood and legitimacy, we learn and reinforce that reality. How might our language change if we re-thought our relationship with the corporate "it"?

- What are McDonalds, Disney, Ben and Jerry's, and Philip Morris? They're all corporations, not people! Yet we speak of them as if they were the guy down the block in that big office building: "Philip Morris refuses to stop selling cigarettes to third world kids." Remember, they're just "legal fictions." So, let's get used to saying the word "corporation" every time we name one. (Give it a try; it's addictive!) Let's also refuse to personify the corporate "it" and instead identify the group or person actually making the decisions. (e.g. "Philip Morris corporation's *directors* are refusing to stop selling cigarettes to third world kids.") Corporations can't demand, want, object, refuse to, etc.; only their directors and shareholders can, because corporations really don't even exist, except on paper (and in our minds)! They are mind-made and they can just as easily be mind-unmade. This distinction helps us stay clear in our thinking about who's real and who's just a toaster. Remember the little man behind the curtain in *The Wizard of Oz*. The Great Oz is merely a projection. Not real at all, though the little man wants us to think otherwise. Same with the corporation! "It" is merely a "legal fiction," i.e. it exists in law but not in the material world in the sense that you cannot take a photograph of "it."

- Let's stop confusing private property and corporate property "rights." The first one is protected by the Bill of Rights. The second one only exists because the corporate "it" won legal personhood in 1886. **Giving corporations property rights is as crazy as saying that racial equality is provided for by giving African Americans separate waiting rooms and lunch counters.** It took 50 years of legal and cultural struggle to reverse the Supreme Court's "separate but equal" decision, and it may take just as long to de-link corporations from "rights" but until we succeed, let's defy corporate "rights" rather than give "it" the respect we do today. If we no longer conceded that corporations had legitimate property "rights," how might this impact our campaigns against them? If we no longer conceded that corporations had legitimate free speech "rights," how might we respond differently to their propaganda?

• Let's stop saying the *privatizing* of electricity, water, etc. It's *corporatizing*, not privatizing. To call it privatizing again accepts that corporate property is private property, which it's not. (Corporations are not "private" entities; they are brought into existence by state governments via Articles of Incorporation.) People have constitutionally protected property *rights*. Corporations only *legitimately* have property *privileges,* as was once stated in their incorporation documents until the late 1800's.

• Corporate doublespeak has infiltrated our daily lives: "conventional food" for example. Translation: the stuff in the supermarket covered in carcinogenic and toxic chemicals (yum!). Imagine participating in a daily act of totally legal civil disobedience. We could start calling "organic food" simply "food" which, until the 1950s was exactly what we *did* call it, and "conventional food" could become … (Oooo, gross! Fill in the blank).

Here are a few more examples, try to think of your own, and then start saying them:

• "Free trade" is really "corporate managed trade."

• We are not merely "protesters," "stakeholders," or "consumers." We are "citizens" or "people" first. Let's stop referring to ourselves with these culturally demeaning terms. The reverse is also true: corporations can't be "good corporate citizens" because they aren't people!

• "Conventional media" and "alternative media." Since this is still officially a democratic republic, and the airwaves are *literally* owned by you and me, why do we call unaccountable corporate-owned media "conventional" and democratically managed and funded media "alternative"? Are we 'We the People' or aren't we? If we are, then let's start calling *our* media "mainstream media," and the other stuff "corporate media." Or even….OMG…. "alternative media"!

- "Workers versus environmentalists" and "jobs versus environment" are phony opposites which pit one group of citizens against another. This is exactly how corporate leaders have designed it, and we shouldn't fall for it. If we *are* going to divide and conquer, how about instead saying "Local communities (workers, environmentalists, etc.) versus absentee corporations."

- "Pirate radio." Why do we call it that when they're simply putting out a radio signal on airwaves *literally* owned by We the People? How about "people's radio" instead, or simply "radio stations"? The real pirates are the media corporations that lease our airwaves for free, sell it back to us through advertising, and monopolize all the frequencies.

- "Defense companies" are really "military corporations," "Forestry companies" are really "forest clear-cutting corporations." And "Health Maintenance Organizations (HMOs)" are really "Dis/ease maintenance organizations (DMOs)." A "Habitat Conservation Plan (HCP)" is really a "Habitat Devastation Plan (HDP)."

Can you think of other phrases invented by corporate propagandists that you've been saying effortlessly for years? Stop that!

I hope this list has amused and alarmed you. I encourage you to expand it via your own life experiences. The long-term goal is to assert our authority as We the People over our subordinate corporate creations. The very first step is to learn to choose our words carefully and consciously, and begin to speak truth about corporate power and authority in all of its dis/guises.

Hidden in Plain Sight:
How Corporations Exercise
Their Constitutional "Rights"
Under Our Very Noses:
A Photography Exhibit

In 2019, I created a traveling photo exhibit to commemorate the Bicentennial of corporations winning constitutional so-called "rights" via the U.S. Supreme Court's "Dartmouth decision" in 1819. Community Rights US made numerous shippable copies of the exhibit and offered them to local activist groups across the country. Throughout that year, many communities displayed the exhibit in coffeehouses, community centers, and public libraries. Many of these communities also held "first night" public events to celebrate the exhibit, timed with their local monthly art gallery walks, which helped to bring in much larger crowds to view it. It's never too late to share this exhibit with the general public. If you think you would enjoy hosting the exhibit in your community, please get in touch with me at Paul@CommunityRights.US. What follows is just a sampling of the full exhibit which contains many more photographs. If you would like to learn more about the significance of that 1819 Supreme Court decision that launched the insane idea that corporations should have constitutional "rights," read my essay titled, "On the Supreme Court's Dartmouth Decision of 1819" which we also encourage you to read aloud at your photo exhibit's opening night event. You can find the essay at www.CommunityRights.US/Book.

We hear more and more these days about large corporations exercising their "personhood" and other so called constitutional "rights." What exactly does it mean for corporations to be exercising constitutional "rights"? Why should the average person even care? Is it something that affects us in our daily lives? YES, it actually does affect us, and much more than you might believe.

While most of us know that corporations spend enormous sums of money to influence our votes and to lobby our elected officials, few of us understand why corporations can do this. The U.S. Supreme Court in 1976 [Buckley v. Valeo] for the first time equated donating money with the "right to speak" and it continues on to the present day. Only because corporations have won a number of Supreme Court decisions giving them access to the First Amendment's free speech guarantee can they speak (spend) so openly. Collectively, these decisions now allow corporations to spend limitless amounts of money to influence every aspect of our electoral system. Beyond that, most of us know very little about how corporations' constitutional "rights" impact us.

This photography exhibit will increase your awareness of how we are impacted by corporations exercising the multitude of constitutional "rights" that the Supreme Court has granted these "artificial persons," which allow corporations to drown us in corporate-designed mass culture, corporate-planned landscapes, corporate-run services, and much more. As Ralph Nader has stated, "We all have one thing in common to start with: We grew up corporate. We look at the world through the filters and lenses and advertisements and messages of the most powerful institution in our country, bar none, which is the modern corporation."

Each photo captures a perfectly normal scene that none of us even notice anymore. We aim to challenge that normalcy, because each photo also captures one aspect of how corporations daily, 24/7, now exercise their constitutional "rights" all around us. We all need to start asking ourselves: can a democratic republic withstand these sorts of subtle but dangerous intrusions into our daily lives? Can "We the People" function democratically when corporations exercise this much control?

Our country wasn't always like this. This history will likely shock you.

Corporations were once required "to obey all laws, to serve the common good, and to cause no harm." We believe such common sense laws need to be implemented again.

Immediately following the American Revolution, corporations were brought into existence one at a time by state legislatures and were literally considered servants of The People. Each entity was required "to obey all laws, to serve the common good, and to cause no harm." Corporate charters (now known as Articles of Incorporation) included many enforceable requirements and prohibitions, including:

- Directors and stockholders held fully liable for all harms and debts

- Unanimous vote of stockholders required for major changes in corporate policy and they were required to live in the state where the corporation was chartered

- Corporations prohibited from owning or merging with other corporations

- Corporations prohibited from donating money or services to influence voters or candidates or elected officials

- Corporations prohibited from donating money or services to civic or charitable organizations

- Corporations permitted to own real estate only to the extent necessary to fulfill their charters

- Corporate accounting books, business records, all considered public information

- Corporations normally chartered for 10 to 30 years, and then charter revoked unless renewed, and charters revocable at any time and for any reason by State Legislature

If the corporate directors significantly violated these rules, the state legislature could dissolve the corporation, seize its assets, and even imprison its directors. In all manners, corporations were legally subordinate to The People.

Are We the People, or aren't we?

Imagine if we still had authority over what corporations were allowed to do. We actually do still have that authority, but we have forgotten our history of who We are, no longer knowing how to exercise our sovereign authority.

We miss our greatest power if we only see our power as consumers who vote with our dollars, or as shareholders who plead for more corporate social responsibility, or as activists who endlessly try to stop one corporate harm at a time. We citizens of these United States are We the People, the Sovereign People. There is no higher authority here than us.

The American Revolution was primarily fought so that commoners, The People, could exercise their inalienable right to local community self-government. It's an opportune time for us to relearn our history and start acting like The People again. The laws that once defined corporations can be renewed. Every one of these historic requirements and prohibitions that ensured that corporations were our servants and not our masters is still worth fighting for.

Community Rights US invites you to explore the hidden history within this exhibit. More importantly, we invite you to join our movement to bring real participatory democracy back to every community. And we encourage you to learn more about our work at www.CommunityRights.US.

WHAT TRANSPIRES WHEN OUR PUBLIC INSTITUTIONS BECOME DEPENDENT ON CORPORATE "GENEROSITY"?

Public highway tollbooth in the Midwest, sponsored by Geico Corporation and Mountain Dew (Pepsi Corporation).

For the first 100 years of our country, it was prohibited for corporations to donate money or services to public institutions because it was understood, both legally and culturally, that We the People must not become dependent on our corporate subordinates. That prohibition no longer exists, which has contributed to the rising influence of corporate actors in the public sphere.

Do your parents and friends ever give you money or help? If so, they probably expect something in return at some point. When corporations no longer pay their fair share of the taxes necessary to support our cherished public institutions and services, such as museums, parks, stadiums, and

Wenatchee, Washington's official directional signs, sponsored by Toyota Corporation.

mass transit-corporations can instead accumulate it as surplus money that they can "donate" to support those same public institutions, which makes those institutions dependent on corporate "generosity."

Today, in this era of ever tightening budgets, most public institutions and government agencies have little choice but to create "partnerships" with large corporations to meet their funding needs. When public entities create these partnerships, what do you suppose corporate directors expect in return for their *donated* money or services? They expect a say in how these public institutions are run. An authentic democratic society cannot survive this slow-motion corporate take-over of our public institutions.

___ ❧ ___

ARE CORPORATIONS TAKING OWNERSHIP OF THE ENGLISH LANGUAGE?

For the first 100 years of our country, only human persons could exercise their intangible property rights such as inventions, trademarks, and copy-rights. It was culturally and legally understood that inventions were owned by the human inventor, not by the inventor's employer. That is no longer the case.

Today, business corporations can exercise intangible property "rights" as corporate persons, and regularly use that constitutionally protected property "right" to trademark entire phrases of the English language. When a corporation trademarks a specific phrase, it literally takes ownership of the English language, and no other person or institution, from then on, is

Above left: First Republic Bank has registered and now owns the phrase "It's a privilege to serve you." Above right: The American Automobile Association (AAA) has applied to the U.S. Government to own the phrase, "Keep life going."

allowed to use that phrase in their own business. We the People all assume that our words, the very language we speak, are part of "the commons" … our public heritage.

Is this corporate ownership of our language acceptable to you?

SHOULD CORPORATE BOARDS OF DIRECTORS BE ALLOWED TO FORMULATE PUBLIC POLICY?

For the first 100 years of our country, corporations were required "to obey all laws, to serve the common good, and to cause no harm." Their entire purpose was defined and legally enforced by state legislatures that wrote their charters. Corporate charters allowed them to be in existence for only one purpose, be it building a bridge or milling grain, and they played no role in making social policy. Today, whether we like it

Coming in for a landing at Los Angeles International Airport. This is what urban land use planning and design look like when the primary decision makers have been corporate leaders from the automobile, oil, and construction industries over the past century. Given that most of us have been raised in corporate landscapes, can We the People even still imagine what an ecologically and socially sustainable urban landscape might look like?

or not, most of us take it for granted that corporate leaders will play an outsized role in formulating public policy.

In the 20th century, the U.S. Supreme Court granted corporations decision-making authority as an intangible property "right" of a corporate person. This has allowed corporate directors to make key decisions that affect all of us—about what corporations will produce and how they will produce it, how they will invest our money, and how to organize their workforce; all with little to no interference from the

The North Carolina Office of Archives and History produced this historical monument in the town of Gastonia about one of the most notable strikes in the labor history of the U.S., and clearly took the side of the Loray Mill Company against its striking employees. Should We the People allow the corporate world view to influence how our history is recorded?

employees (unionized or not), the public, or the government. Corporations are allowed to exercise this "right" regardless of who or what gets harmed as a result: our water, our air, our health, our environment, or our communities. That is, the Supreme Court has decided that corporations have the "rights" of flesh-and-blood people, but not the responsibilities. As a result, for example, corporate boardrooms get to decide that the society will run on coal and oil rather than renewable energy, which is now causing a climate emergency. That wasn't a government decision. And it wasn't a decision that any of us had any input to. It was purely a corporate decision.

But that's not all. Corporate leaders now claim the mantle of leading visionaries, urging the public to follow their wise approaches. Is this the kind of society we want future generations to experience?

ARE CORPORATE TRADE SECRETS DANGEROUS?

For the first 100 years of our country, corporations were prohibited from keeping any trade secrets. "Proprietary information" was not yet considered a privacy "right" of a corporate person. That is no longer the case.

Do you ever look at the ingredients label on pesticide and insecticide products only to notice how little is actually revealed in those labels? Currently, by exercising their corporate "right" of privacy, corporations are able to sell products without disclosing everything that is in them, and we citizens have no right to demand that information. This corporate "right" threatens the safety of our families, pets and the land. The next time you make such a purchase in a hardware store or plant nursery, ask yourself whether you think it should be legal for companies to sell products that are almost entirely made from unlabeled trade secret ingredients.

At left: Round-Up Weed & Grass Killer (manufactured by Monsanto Corp) contains 96% proprietary (trade secret) ingredients. At right: Bayer Corp's Rose & Flower Insect Killer contains 99.997% "other ingredients." In other words, they only have to tell you what's in that remaining .003% (or 3/1000th's) of their product, because the corporation has the constitutionally-protected "right" to hide this information from the public as a trade secret.

CAN CIVIL SOCIETY SURVIVE ANY MORE CORPORATE FUNDING OF NON-PROFIT ORGANIZATIONS?

For the first 100 years of our country, it was understood both legally and culturally, that the sovereign people must not become dependent on their corporate subordinates. The people knew that corporate directors could not

The Nature Conservancy is a massive tax-exempt educational non-profit organization, with $1.29 billion in annual revenues, led and funded by giant corporations. Its board of directors includes the current or former CEOs of Dow Chemical Company, JP Morgan Chase, Duke Energy and others.

Can a major environmental organization really succeed at protecting the environment when their primary funders' impact is the poisoning of our world? The next time you see this slogan on their marketing, give it a little added dose of honesty: "United by Nature. Guided by Science. Led and Funded by Giant Industrial and Banking Corporations."

The Breast Cancer Research Foundation (BCRF) is a major educational nonprofit organization founded by a corporate executive from The Estee Lauder Companies Inc, a multinational manufacturer and marketer of skincare, makeup, fragrance, and hair care products. Some of its products have long been suspected of causing cancer. Other major funders of the BCRF include Delta Airlines and Minute Maid Company (owned by The Coca-Cola Company). These two corporations remind the airline passengers of their corporate commitment to the funding of the BCRF.

be trusted to participate rationally in public decision-making because corporate self-interest would take over and negate the public interest. So it was a felony for corporations to donate money or services to non-profit organizations. This is no longer the case, because corporate lawyers fought for decades in the courts to end this corporate prohibition.

Today, very few non-profit organizations refrain from accepting massive corporate donations (Community Rights US is a rare exception) and those donations impact an organization's goals and tactics. For example, no large non-profit organizations launch major campaigns that their corporate benefactors oppose even if such campaigns serve the public interest. No non-profit directors cry foul when their corporate benefactors are implicated in serious corporate crimes because they are entirely dependent on the "generosity" of corporations to pay their bills. And finally, non-profit goals have become less daring as they are subject to corporate approval.

The BCRF and other so-called "war on cancer" organizations receive massive annual donations from many other corporations that cause significant environmental harm (including cancer) such as Bee Sweet Citrus Corporation, which sprays its mandarin oranges with three chemicals that are all known or suspected carcinogens. It's not cancer that needs to be attacked, it's the root causes of cancer, which are primarily the entirely legal poisoning of our air, our water, and our food by large corporations. If we really want to tackle the cancer epidemic in this country, we need to start by passing community rights laws that strip corporations of their constitutional so-called "right" to poison us.

WHEN TRUTH IS STRANGER THAN FICTION

For the first 100 years of our country, corporations had not yet been granted "personhood" status by the U.S. Supreme Court, and thus exercised none of the rights of persons listed in the amendments to the U.S. Constitution. This began to change in 1886, when the Supreme Court recognized corporations as persons under the 14th Amendment, granting them equal protection and due process. The 14th Amendment had been intended to provide this protection to enslaved African men, not corporations.

Corporations were later granted First Amendment free speech "rights" by the U.S. Supreme Court for the first time in 1936. They explicitly won the right of both "political speech" and "commercial speech" as First Amendment protected rights in separate Supreme Court cases in 1976: meaning that a corporation could now participate in the society with its own voice, including: political lobbying, campaign donations, public participation in policy discussions, commercial advertising, etc. Nike Corporation's lawyers even attempted in 2003 to get the Supreme Court to recognize a corporation's "right" to lie (as a subset of its "right" to speak) but so far the company has failed.

Today, even the corporate junk mail that we all receive at home in our mail boxes is given the status of First Amendment protected corporate speech, thus you and I are not permitted to opt out from receiving this instant garbage as it would violate the corporate person's "right" to speak to us.

You too can celebrate "National Small Business Week" at Staples, the multinational corporation with 1200 stores in the U.S. alone. It also owns Corporate Express Inc, one of the world's largest office supply wholesalers. In 2017, Staples Corp was bought by Sycamore Partners for $6.9 billion. Small business indeed!

Subway restaurant windows announce hot chicken sandwiches with "Fried Flavor Baked Right In"!

Let's Start Thinking
About "Law"
In a Whole New Way

I wrote this as a commentary/podcast for the KBOO Evening News in Portland, Oregon on January 13, 2015.

Today I want to talk about law. For most Americans, law is that scary thing that police and the courts use to cause you great suffering, either in prison or with massive fines that most of us cannot afford, and more often than not for crimes that are victimless and where no one was hurt, like being caught with a small amount of marijuana.

A huge percentage of Americans are sitting in prison today for such crimes, which, in my opinion, is an obscenity. In states where the judges are required to follow the outrageous "three strikes and you're out" sentencing rules, additional massive numbers of Americans are in prison with long sentences, or even life sentences, because their third and final crime was sometimes nothing more serious than stealing a slice of pizza. **Yes, we certainly are a nation of laws, but what kind of a nation of laws are we? We are a nation of unjust laws. We are a nation of selectively enforced laws. We are a nation of unquestioned and unchallenged laws.**

There's a quote I love, by Anatole France, a French poet, journalist and novelist, born in 1844, which says, "How noble the law, in its majestic equality, that both the rich and poor are equally prohibited from peeing in the streets, sleeping under bridges, and stealing bread!"

Ally Fogg, a British writer and journalist describes the Anatole France quote perfectly, when he writes, "To treat rich and poor alike is to treat them entirely differently." What an interesting thing to try to get your head around.

Imagine living in a society where there were no extremes of rich and poor. In such a society, it's likely that very few people would steal from other people because everyone would have enough of what they needed to thrive. So, laws about theft would likely only rarely, if ever, be used.

In May of 2014, I met an extraordinary legal scholar from Victoria, Canada at a conference. Her name is Val Napoleon. She's an Indigenous woman who teaches law at the University of Victoria in British Columbia, where she is the director of the Indigenous Law Research Unit. Val Napoleon taught me something that blew my mind.

In our western culture, activists tend to refer to laws that are unfair or oppressive as "unjust laws" or "illegitimate laws," and they work hard to get rid of these laws. It turns out that in historical Indigenous societies, laws that were unjust or illegitimate were not even considered law at all. In fact, there were eight legal requirements that a law had to meet for it to be considered a law at all within an Indigenous community. Indigenous people were non-state, decentralized societies, so law did not come from formal, central state processes. Instead, law originated from the Indigenous citizens themselves. Law was about relational commitments. It had to fulfill specific needs or requirements of that community. Val Napoleon and her colleagues are working with many Indigenous communities across Canada to restate and rebuild historical legal understandings, returning them to what I call "background normal."

Try to imagine what your community might look like, might feel like, if the only laws that existed there were ones where the entire community had an active role in creating or at least approving. Imagine living in a community where laws that oppressed certain classes of people would not even exist as law, because they failed to meet the definition of what a law is. I do a lot of teaching all over this country about some very bold and ambitious ideas about democracy and law, and it's hard, even for me, to imagine what my community would look and feel like in that situation.

In virtually every city in this country, if you want to buy a standard lot and build a whole bunch of micro-homes for you and your friends to live in community together, you would be breaking the law. If you wanted to take responsibility by keeping your poop out of the water supply and instead compost it on-site, you would be breaking the law. If you and your neighbors wanted to tear up the entire street in front of your homes and plant food gardens there instead, you would be breaking the law.

If your neighborhood wanted to dismantle the existing centralized sewer system, and instead treat and use the greywater within the neighborhood, you would be breaking the law. If the residents of your town or city decided to dismantle the existing centralized electricity grid and replace it with a decentralized solar and wind system, you would be breaking the law. No wonder that very few of us ever seriously consider doing these sorts of activities, even though none of these activities would hurt anyone, and in fact, would be an improvement in everyone's lives.

Why do we put up with laws that have been imposed upon us from above?

In this country, we take it for granted that laws are something we have almost no control over, and therefore, very few of us ever imagine doing anything to overrule or overthrow an unjust law. Instead, we try to hide our own violations of existing laws, and we work hard not to get caught. That's a pretty good definition right there of a people who feel powerless in their own communities. Yet, we call this democracy?!

Why do we put up with laws that have been imposed upon us from above? Why do we allow laws to remain in place that do not serve us, and that were written by people who have been dead for a very long time?

Now, allow me to flip this question upside down.

Why is it totally legal, under our existing system of law, for a corporation to pour toxic and cancer-causing chemicals endlessly into the air and water as part of its manufacturing process? And at the same time, why is it illegal, under our existing system of law, for the people of a city or town to pass a law that bans (rather than regulates) the ongoing poisoning of our air and water by corporations? Or more generally, why are most ecologically sustainable practices illegal, and unsustainable practices, not only legal, but required by law? Would it not make a heck of a lot more sense if those activities that were ecologically unsustainable, or economically and socially unjust, were simply made illegal? An impressive group that's tackling one aspect of this problem is Recode (www.RecodeNow.org) which develops, promotes, and helps to get adopted the codes and local ordinances that create a more sustainable relationship with our water.

I am involved as a teacher and community organizer in the community rights movement because I am convinced that the time has arrived for We the People to get ourselves organized and mobilized to oppose and dismantle unjust and illegitimate laws that violate our inherent right to govern goal is to dismantle unjust structures of law at all levels of the society, so that the law serves all of us, rather than just a tiny percentage of us.

Imagine your community ten years from now, where people have joined together to redefine law itself, where the only laws that still exist are those that meet everyone's needs. Now that's something I'll bet we could all get excited about!

Chapter Two

Situation Urgent:
Life in the Balance

Corporations decide how our food is grown and distributed,
how we heat and light our homes, how we travel,
what poisons we breathe and drink and eat.
They decide who works, doing what, how wealth is shared,
what controversies get attention, what analyses and solutions are acceptable,
who gets elected to public office, how this nation treats other nations. Why?

– Richard Grossman
Co-Founder, Program on Corporations, Law and Democracy

We the People
Standing Together
to Protect Our Climate:
Lessons from the
Community Rights Movement

*I presented this speech to the people of Saint Paul, Minnesota, on February 23, 2015. The event was sponsored by the Minnesota chapter of 350.org, Idle No More, Honor the Earth, the Minnesota Green Party and many other groups. I used Naomi Klein's extraordinary book, **This Changes Everything**, as the jumping off point for the speech, proposing the community rights strategy as the critical missing piece in Naomi's book. Naomi's vision begs for a community rights solution. David Barsamian then broadcast a much shorter version of my speech to his nationally syndicated Alternative Radio audience. I gave this speech again, in Portland, Oregon, on May 14, 2015. You can watch it in its entirety as well as the extensive Q&A session at www.CommunityRights.US/Book.*

We are here tonight to think about climate change. I've never liked the term because it makes it sound like just another environmental problem to add to the already existing pile of problems. And hey, it can't be that bad, right? We'll end up with a longer growing season for our crops and less ice on the roads.

So, I prefer to call it catastrophic climate destabilization. Somehow, that term wakes me up rather than lulls me back into passivity.

Here are my goals for the evening.

- To convince you that there actually are some very powerful things that all of you can do about the climate crisis, that you may never have even thought of doing;

- To get you to think about yourself more as an active citizen and less as a single-issue activist;

- To ask you to question some of the assumptions you may be making about what the proper relationship is between yourself and your government;

- And, oh yeah, one more not insignificant thing: I am going to be proposing tonight perhaps **the most ambitious expansion of community self-governance since the American Revolution.** Hold on to your hats!

So that we're all on the same page, let's review what scientists are telling us is likely to happen with increasing frequency on our planet if we don't respond boldly and quickly to the catastrophic climate destabilization. Before I read you the list I want to ask you to try to listen, not just with your head but with your whole body. Allow whatever feelings may arise, and remember to breathe.

Extreme heat waves, declining global food stocks, collapse of entire ecosystems, sea levels rising, huge hurricanes, raging wildfires, collapse of ocean fisheries and coral reefs, widespread disruptions to water supplies, mass extinctions of plant and animal species, wide-ranging droughts, globe-trotting diseases, super typhoons, collapsing ice shelves and retreating glaciers, significant changes in precipitation, rapid ocean acidification, thawing of permafrost, collapse of animal reproduction.

In preparation for tonight's talk, I just finished reading Naomi Klein's breathtaking new book, *This Changes Everything.* In a nutshell, it's about how the climate crisis can only be solved if we change everything about the way we are living on planet Earth, and that nothing short of the largest pro-democracy mobilization in the history of the world is going to be required to resolve this crisis. I couldn't agree more. I only wish that Naomi Klein was aware of the community rights movement when she wrote the book, because the proposals she makes could best be instituted by a rights-based movement working first at the local level. I plan to send her a copy of this speech and see if we might be able to recruit her! And in the meantime, I urge you to find a copy of her book, and read it cover to cover. It's a terrific read.

Here's an excerpt from the introduction to the book:

I denied climate change for longer than I care to admit. I knew it was happening, sure. Not like Donald Trump and the Tea Partiers going on about how the continued existence of winter proves it's all a hoax. But I stayed pretty hazy on the details and only skimmed most of the news stories, especially the really scary ones. I told myself the science was too complicated and that the environmentalists were dealing with it. And I continued to behave as if there was nothing wrong with the shiny card in my wallet attesting to my "elite" frequent flyer status.

A great many of us engage in this kind of climate change denial. We look for a split second and then we look away. Or we look but then turn it into a joke ("more signs of the apocalypse!"). Which is another way of looking away.

Or we look but tell ourselves comforting stories about how humans are clever and will come up with a technological miracle that will safely suck the carbon out of the skies or magically turn down the heat of the sun. Which ... is yet another way of looking away.

Or we look but try to be hyper-rational about it ("dollar for dollar it's more efficient to focus on economic development than climate change, since wealth is the best protection from weather extremes") as if having a few more dollars will make much difference when your city is underwater. Which is a way of looking away if you happen to be a policy wonk.

Or we look but tell ourselves we are too busy to care about something so distant and abstract even though we saw the water in the subways in New York City, and the people on their rooftops in New Orleans, and know that no one is safe, the most vulnerable least of all. And though perfectly understandable, this too is a way of looking away.

Or we look but tell ourselves that all we can do is focus on ourselves. Meditate and shop at farmers' markets and stop driving but forget trying to actually change the systems that are making the crisis inevitable because that's too much "bad energy" and it will never work. And at first it may appear as if we are looking, because many of these lifestyle changes are indeed part of the solution, but we still have one eye tightly shut.

Or maybe we do look, really look, but then, inevitably we seem to forget. Remember and then forget again. Climate change is like that; it's hard to keep it in your head for very long. We engage in this odd form of on-again-off-again ecological amnesia for perfectly rational reasons. We deny because we fear that letting in the full reality of this crisis will change everything. And we are right.

We know that if we continue on our current path of allowing emissions to rise year after year, climate change will change everything about our world. And we don't have to do anything to bring about this future. All we have to do is nothing. Just continue to do what we are doing now, whether it's counting on a techno-fix or tending to our gardens or telling ourselves we're unfortunately too busy to deal with it.

All we have to do is not react as if this is a full-blown crisis. All we have to do is keep on denying how frightened we actually are. And then, bit by bit, we will have arrived at the place we most fear, the thing from which we have been averting our eyes. No additional effort required.

There are ways of preventing this grim future, or at least making it a lot less dire. But the catch is that these also involve changing everything.

So, I ask myself, what exactly would it look like for us to change everything here in the United States, at a time when our nation more and more resembles a corporate oligarchy with each passing month? Clearly, transforming our society so that it becomes truly sustainable isn't going to happen overnight, and yet we really don't have much of a grace period either. As you have probably already heard, the scientific consensus is that we absolutely have to keep the planet's warming trend to below the target of two degrees Celsius, which will require the world's wealthy countries to cut their emissions by somewhere in the neighborhood of 8 to 10% a year. So, that means we need to start this year! In the past, this level of emission reduction has happened only in the context of economic collapse or deep depressions.

In my opinion, the very first and most important task on our grand to-do list is to stop lying to ourselves about what's really going on with our government, and why it's doing such a lousy job of responding to our needs and protecting our rights. Let me tell you what I see when I look at the activism that is taking place day after day across this country. It's not pretty.

Every day, I am bombarded by emails and articles and news stories that all make the same assumption. Most of my politically active friends make this same assumption. Virtually all of the environmental and labor and social justice organizations in the country make the same assumption. It's an assumption that I don't think is true.

What is the assumption? It's that we live in a society that was designed to function democratically, but has been overtaken by greedy corporate leaders and corrupt politicians. That we simply have to push back on corporate power, elect better people to public office, and things will start to function well again. How can I tell that all of these people and groups are making this assumption? It's actually surprisingly easy. I simply watch their activism.

For example, if you were to live in a society where the government and its structures of law were truly designed to serve We the People, then your activism would closely match the activism we see all around us. You would vote. You would work within the regulatory process to show your concerns about what corporations were doing regarding agriculture, forestry, labor, energy, commerce, and media. When the political class was making decisions that you were convinced were the wrong ones, you would sign online petitions, you would march and rally in front of government or corporate offices, you would write submissions for or testify at public hearings organized by state and federal regulatory agencies, you would take corporations or government to court when the people's will was not being served. That's basically the sort of activism that I notice is happening all around me, where people generally appear to believe that the system is there to serve them, or they wouldn't keep doing what they're doing. Right?

On the other hand, if you were to live in a society where the government and its structures of law were designed to serve the ruling elite, you would already understand that working within the existing system of government would not get you the desired results. You would already understand that your elected officials, at least those at the state and federal level, are there to serve the ruling elite, not you, so it's unlikely that you would plead with them to do the right thing. You would already understand that the courts are generally rigged in favor of the 1%, so you would have very low expectations about the courts ruling in your favor.

In this situation, it's quite likely that you would feel so frustrated and angry and powerless that you would probably be completely turned off to the official processes available to you, which I believe explains the behavior of the vast majority of us in this country.

Or, it's also possible that you would see through the mirage of allowable activism, and would still choose to participate, but your activism would follow very different contours, which describes the behavior of a significant minority of us in this country.

In either of these last two scenarios, you would already understand that the regulatory agencies are also not what they appear to be. To the untrained eye, it may look like the government has appointed officials who take the public's concerns very seriously before making their decisions. But in fact, the entire structure of regulatory law was designed behind closed doors with leaders of the railroad industry in the 1880s as a new and clever way to keep the public as far as possible from where the actual decisions were being made. When the system was first implemented, it worked so well for the railroad industry that one industry after another demanded its own regulatory agency. If you already understood all of this, you would choose to not play the game, because you would realize that, by design, the system was rigged. Not broken. Rigged!

Our system of government was actually designed, right from the start, to serve the elite.

But here's the kicker. Virtually every activist group in this country today is playing this rigged game. They're packing regulatory hearings. They're marching and rallying on single issue after single issue. They're suing government agencies and corporations. They're signing endless online petitions to government and corporate leaders.

The various movements that are active in this country to protect our climate are doing exactly the same kinds of activism. No wonder our climate crisis is getting worse and worse and worse.

What the heck is going on? The conclusion that I have come to is that most of us really do believe that if we keep doing the same thing we are currently doing, somehow the results are going to be different in the future than they have been in the past. That somehow, if we just pack one more public hearing about oil trains, or if we can collect 50,000 signatures to beg the governor to stop the latest mine, then finally our leaders will see the light. This is the behavior of a person whose mind has been colonized. We the People of the United States of America have been fed a big lie, and we've bought it, hook line and sinker. I know we have because our activism strategies prove it.

Our government is doing a lousy job of serving our needs. Everyone knows that. But it's not because greedy corporate leaders and corrupt politicians stole our democracy. It's because our system of government was actually designed, right from the start, to serve the elite, and it has been working quite well ever since. James Madison was the primary drafter of the current U.S. Constitution. He believed that the new constitutional system had to be designed so as to ensure that the government will "protect the minority of the opulent against the majority." Those are James Madison's words.

The founding fathers were determined that the nation would not operate as a functioning democracy. That's why the U.S. Constitution says nothing about the rights of people. It's all about property and commerce. The Bill of Rights and the other amendments were added later, because the rabble — that's us — were outraged about what was left out.

In modern law, if you want to look at one of the places where elite rule is functioning exceptionally well, you need look no further than our regulatory agencies. There are a breathtaking number of them!

Their function hasn't changed much since the 1880s. Regulatory agencies regulate corporate behavior. The only problem is that the agencies are run by the industries that regulate them. The agency directors tend to be in revolving doors with their industries. Regulatory law is written by those who are regulated. You couldn't make this stuff up!

You may be shocked to realize how many departments of our government, that most people believe are serving us, are actually run by the captains of industry. Here is a sampling.

At the federal level, there's the Environmental Protection Agency, and the National Labor Relations Board, and the Food and Drug Administration, and the Department of Agriculture, and the Federal Communications Commission, and the Department of Energy, and the Federal Deposit Insurance Corporation, and the Federal Trade Commission, and the Interstate Commerce Commission, and the Nuclear Regulatory Commission, and the Occupational Safety and Health Administration, among others.

In Minnesota you've got the Pollution Control Agency, and the Department of Agriculture, and the Board of Animal Health, and the Minnesota Department of Commerce, and the Department of Labor and Industry, and the Department of Natural Resources, among others.

So, let's say you're a Minnesota resident concerned about catastrophic climate destabilization. Well, you would probably contact your state or federal Department of Agriculture to let them know that you want fossil fuel-based fertilizers and pesticides to be banned. Or you may think it's a good idea to contact the Federal Communications Commission to ask them to stop oil and gas corporations from drowning our airwaves in lies about renewable energy. Or you might be told to contact the Minnesota Department of Natural Resources to urge them to stop allowing dangerous oil trains on the rail lines that pass through your community.

Do you see the problem with this scenario? You will have just spent a lot of your time and energy interacting with a structure of law that is entirely run by the corporations, and for the benefit of the corporations. You are on their playing field. You are playing by their rules. You have already lost the game. No wonder the climate crisis just keeps getting worse.

I have been teaching and organizing about community versus corporate "rights" for almost 20 years now, and when I talk about this in my workshops, I'm always impressed by how many folks experience a huge wave of relief. Many folks say to me, "No wonder it always seems like such an uphill battle to get our leaders to listen to us. Now I finally get it why a public hearing on mining or fracking or oil trains or big box stores could be filled to capacity by local residents opposed to the corporate plan, but the plan would get approved anyway." People would tell me that this new information was like a breath of fresh air for them, that finally they can stop blaming themselves for the endless failures to stop one corporate atrocity after another.

As we start to realize that our assumptions are not true about how our government really operates, the waking up begins. The process of letting go of our assumptions can take some serious twists and turns, as we acknowledge to ourselves and to those around us that our leaders are not actually our leaders after all. This painful realization can come as quite a blow to our

psyches, and we may need to allow ourselves some time to grieve, to feel angry, or depressed.

My colleague and friend, Betsy Barnum, says that the current structure of law keeps "We the People docile, passive, and even hopeless." She says,

> When we can see through the current system and how it has deliberately disempowered us, something wakes up inside, at least potentially. The lid comes off the box. Limitations on our own capacities such as creativity and imagination, limitations that we assumed were natural and permanent, get released, and all kinds of things are possible that were never possible before, simply because we couldn't see them due to being inside that box.
>
> As we learn to contradict the story

> ...that we are selfish, greedy and violent by nature, [it] opens up another whole, vast field of possibility for creating together, trying what we can do and make when we join our capacities together for the sake of the greater good of our communities. This shift in perspective has the potential to truly be both revolutionary and evolutionary.

This perspective is exciting to me on many levels because once we come to terms with the fact that we're living in a "Democracy Theme Park," (Jane Anne Morris: www.DemocracyThemePark.org) we realize that there are lots of levers and foot pedals, but that not one of them is connected to anything real. Then we can begin to imagine a different kind of citizen participation where we no longer give our power away as We the People, but we instead devise systems and structures of law where the levers and foot pedals are attached to something real. I tend to refer to that real something as self-governing authority. Very few of us even know what those words mean. For some, those words may be just as scary as the current hall of mirrors. But for me, it's more hopeful than anything else that I can imagine!

I want to live in a society where the decisions are being made by the people who are most directly impacted by those decisions. To me, that's self-governing authority. And that's what the community rights movement is all about.

I have been doing this work since 1997, helping communities to learn how to rein in corporate constitutional so-called "rights" and enshrine the community's right to govern itself, through a new and very bold kind of law making. What I continue to witness is that there is more ripeness in this country today than I have ever seen before. By ripeness, I mean a willingness to let go of some very large assumptions about how we are supposed to live, both as citizens of this country and of Mother Earth. I see a real readiness to participate directly in those dramatic changes. Today, people are more prepared to abandon conventional activism than I have ever witnessed in my many decades of social movement work.

I want to urge those of you who are active to not give up on the huge majority of Americans who aren't. These people aren't apathetic. They are waiting for something that actually addresses the reality of the current state of our institutions. And, boy oh boy, do we need to see big changes in that department! Our so-called leaders clearly aren't leading, so we need a new plan.

Here's another excerpt from the introduction to Naomi Klein's new book, *This Changes Everything*:

Climate change has never received the crisis treatment from our leaders, despite the fact that it carries the risk of destroying lives on a vastly greater scale than collapsed banks or collapsed buildings. The cuts to our greenhouse gas emissions that scientists tell us are necessary in order to greatly reduce the risk of catastrophe are treated as nothing more than gentle suggestions, actions that can be put off pretty much indefinitely. Clearly, what gets declared a crisis is an expression of power and priorities as much as hard facts. But we need not be spectators in all this: politicians aren't the only ones with the power to declare a crisis. Mass movements of regular people can declare one too.

Slavery wasn't a crisis for British and American elites until abolitionists turned it into one ... Racial discrimination wasn't a crisis until the civil rights movement turned it into one ... Sex discrimination wasn't a crisis until feminism turned it into one ... Apartheid wasn't a crisis until the anti-apartheid movement turned it into one.

In the very same way, if enough of us stop looking away and decide that climate change is a crisis worthy of Marshall Plan levels of response, then it will become one.

Naomi Klein goes on to say that through conversations with others in the growing climate justice movement, she began to see all kinds of ways that climate change could become a catalyzing force for positive change, how it could be the best argument we citizens have ever had to insist on fundamental changes to how our society functions, and who is in charge. This point is further developed by Miya Yoshitani, executive director of the Oakland, California-based Asian Pacific Environmental Network, when she says,

> The climate justice fight here in the U.S. and around the world is not just a fight against the [biggest] ecological crisis of all time. It is the fight for a new economy, a new energy system, a new democracy, a new relationship to the planet and to each other, for land, water, and food sovereignty, for Indigenous rights, for human rights and dignity for all people. When climate justice wins, we win the world that we want. We can't sit this one out, not because we have too much to lose but because we have too much to gain ... We are bound together in this battle, not just for a reduction in the parts per million of CO2, but to transform our economies and rebuild a world that we want today.

When I look at the community rights movement's growth over the past 15 years, and when I look at the cultural changes that are so urgently required to tackle the climate crisis, what I see is a match made in heaven. **I am absolutely convinced that the climate crisis can best be addressed not at the federal level, not at the state level, but at the local level, at least initially.** What we need to build is a massive democracy movement, of towns, cities, and counties declaring their right to govern themselves, and to pass local laws that transform them into ecologically sustainable and socially just places, with the bold goal of becoming entirely fossil-fuel free within the next few decades. This is the stuff that gets me so darn excited.

Let me give you a brief snapshot of the community rights movement. It started in the very small rural conservative farm community of Wells Township, Pennsylvania, which had grown weary of trying to stop a factory farm corporation from placing 15,000 hogs in its township. The farmers were using the only political process that they had been told was an option: pleading with a regulatory agency, the Pennsylvania Department of Agriculture. Once they realized that regulatory agencies allow and regulate corporate activities, rather than prohibit them, regardless of what the community wants, they took the incredibly courageous step of passing a local law that *banned* factory farms. This was illegal and unconstitutional under our existing structures of law.

It was illegal because it violated state pre-emption and Dillon's Rule, which both limit the power and authority of local self-government. It was unconstitutional because it violated the factory farm corporation's so-called constitutional "rights." This is the playing field that U.S. communities find themselves in because of a number of outrageous structures of law that prohibit local elected leaders from protecting the health and welfare of the communities they have pledged to serve.

The Wells Township supervisors decided that they cared more about defending the health and welfare of their small community, than they worried about the consequences of breaking an unjust law. In fact, the corporation pulled its application and went elsewhere.

Within a few years, 20 rural conservative farm communities in Pennsylvania had passed identical laws, banning non-family-owned corporations from engaging in farming or owning farmland. That's how the community rights movement began, in 1999, in a small township of about 500 people. Fast forward 15 years, and there are now about 200 communities and counties in nine states that have passed community rights laws. Each local rights-based law accomplishes three extraordinary things:

- It prohibits a specific corporate activity that is currently legal and is therefore regulated under state or federal law, but which the local community considers too harmful to allow, such as fracking, factory farms, large-scale water withdrawals, sludge dumping, oil trains, GMO agriculture, etc.

- It strips that particular sector of corporations of all of its so-called constitutional "rights."

- It enshrines the right of a local town, city, or county, to pass whatever laws it believes are required, to protect the health and welfare of the human and non-human residents of that local place.

These laws have been passed in Pennsylvania, New Hampshire, Maine, New York, Maryland, Ohio, Colorado, New Mexico, and California. They are locally enforceable and all stopped significant corporate harm dead in its tracks.

In New Hampshire, in response to a proposed high-voltage transmission line from Quebec, a handful of small towns have passed locally enforceable Right to Sustainable Energy Future ordinances that would prohibit any corporate activity that meets their local definition of "unsustainable energy systems." Intriguingly, even industrial wind power would be banned in these communities, unless it was "locally or municipally owned and operated."

Across a number of states, many small towns, as well as the city of Pittsburgh, Pennsylvania, have passed Right to Water ordinances that ban fracking. Mendocino County, California, passed their fracking ban this past November, becoming the first community rights ordinance ever to become law in the state of California.

In Benton County, Oregon, on May 19, 2015, voters had the opportunity to pass a law that would ban all GMO agriculture in the county. (Update: it passed.) Their local ordinance was designed to establish a locally enforceable Right to a Local Food System, a Right to Seed Heritage, a Right to Self-Government, as well as Rights of Natural Communities.

And in Columbia County, Oregon, the local community rights group plans to ask voters later this year to pass an ordinance that would ban all oil and gas trains through their county. It would also ban any fossil fuel exports to China from their local port on the Columbia River. It would enshrine into law, among other things, a Right to Climate, and a Right to Local Community Self-Government.

These are just a few of the 200 communities in those nine states that have passed these ordinances in the past 15 years. Ninety-five percent of these communities have never been challenged in court. The Community Environmental Legal Defense Fund pioneered this legally ground-breaking work. Until recently, I worked in partnership with this very impressive group, and am now in the process of setting up a brand-new national community rights support organization that will soon be offering a second option for local communities that wish to launch community rights ordinance campaigns. This organization will provide training in organizing, campaign support, and how to sustain a group over many years, as well as legal support in the writing and defending of a community rights ordinance. (Update: We launched Community Rights US in 2017.)

Imagine …

We could stop pleading with our government and corporate leaders to protect us, and instead start passing local laws that set enforceable standards that could take us to a post-fossil-fuel economy. We could stop begging our senators and congress people to vote no on fast track authority for the latest global corporate trade treaty outrage like the Trans-Pacific so-called Partnership and instead pass local laws that nullify the enforceability of this treaty within the boundaries of our communities.

Over the next few years, as the so-called leaders from all over the world meet yet again to discuss how to respond to the climate crisis, there could already be hundreds and then thousands of American communities leaping past the deadlocked climate negotiations, drastically cutting their own local carbon emissions, and moving towards creating carbon-neutral communities within the next few decades.

You think I'm being unrealistic? Frankfurt and Munich, Germany, have pledged to move to 100% renewable electricity by 2050 and 2025, respectively. Germany gets way less sun than does much of the U.S. and yet its government is aiming for 55-60% renewables by 2035, just 20 years from now. If Germany can do it, so can we!

In fact, many communities and entire countries are moving forward now with very ambitious cuts in carbon emissions, some through policy, others through effective nonviolent direct action. Some of them are: Greenburg, Kansas; Austin, Texas; Sacramento, California; the State of New York; and the countries of Greece, Denmark, Nigeria, Costa Rica, and France.

Many studies exist showing that wealthy countries can shift all, or almost all, of their electricity-generating infrastructure to renewables within a 20 to 40-year time frame. One of the studies offered a groundbreaking detailed roadmap for how 100% of the world's energy, for all purposes, could be supplied by wind, water, and solar resources by as early as 2030. The plan includes not only power generation but also transportation as well as heating and cooling. (I must say that I am extremely skeptical about some of these claims.)

Mark Jacobson, who co-authored the study that was published in 2013 in the journal Energy Policy, says,

This really involves a large-scale transformation. It would require an effort comparable to the Apollo moon project or constructing the interstate highway system. But it is possible, without even having to go to new technologies. We really need to just decide collectively that this is the direction we want to head as a society.

There have been two main stumbling blocks here in the U.S. The first is that, decade after decade, our so-called leaders have had other priorities.

The second stumbling block I have already discussed, that We the People have continued to wait, decade after decade, for our federal government to act decisively, while we've continued to march and rally and demand and plead and beg. Clearly, it's time to try something else. Clearly, our leaders are not our leaders after all. Perhaps we are the leaders we've been waiting for!

Naomi Klein reminds us that, "During extraordinary historical moments, both world wars, the aftermath of the Great Depression, or the peak of the civil rights era, the usual categories dividing 'activists' and 'regular people' became meaningless because the project of changing society was so deeply woven in the project of life. Activists were, quite simply, everyone."

We are certainly not there yet, nor are we even close. What I do believe is that a community rights approach to this crisis could dramatically change this equation in our favor.

I'm guessing that, by now, some of you must be thinking that it would be pretty darn likely that large corporations would sue communities that passed such bold ordinances, or that the state would never allow it in the first place.

In response, let me ask you a question:

Which of these scenarios is more frightening to you: your community getting sued for protecting itself? Or the consequences of catastrophic climate destabilization making our planet uninhabitable for our species in the future?

I'll repeat that question:

Which of these scenarios is more frightening to you: your community getting sued for protecting itself? Or the consequences of catastrophic climate destabilization making our planet uninhabitable for our species in the future?

It should be obvious by now how those 200 communities in nine states answered that question, the ones that have already passed legally ground-breaking community rights ordinances that enshrine local self-governing authority and ban harmful corporate activities. All of these communities knew they were breaking the law, but they proceeded anyway, because they valued the rights of their own communities over the so-called constitutional "rights" of corporations. **We call this form of local law-making an act of municipal civil disobedience.**

Let's not forget what the purpose of a real government is. It's right there at the very beginning of every state constitution. The language is a remnant from the American Revolution. Here's how the Minnesota State Constitution begins:

> **Article One: Bill of Rights**
> **Section One: Object of Government**
> Government is instituted for the security, benefit, and pro-
> tection of the people, … in whom all political power is
> inherent, … together with the right to alter, modify or reform
> government … whenever required by the public good.

In other words, government exists to serve us! It's instituted to protect us! All political power is inherent in We the People. That's us! And if government isn't serving us, we have the authority to make whatever changes are necessary in government to serve the public good. The language could not be clearer! And really, if you think about it, that's all these 200 communities are doing!

Here's a quote from Abraham Lincoln, saying pretty much the same thing. He spoke these words in 1861 on his very first day in office as President:

> This country, with its institutions, belongs to the people who
> inhabit it. Whenever they shall grow weary of the existing
> government, they can exercise their constitutional right of
> amending it, or their revolutionary right to dismember or
> overthrow it.

What an extraordinarily brave thing for a president to say! Now this guy was a real leader!

What would it look like, what would it feel like, if we Americans really started to believe these words again? How might that impact our capacity individually and collectively, to shift our behavior from activist to citizen?

All great social movements started somewhere local. For example, the abolitionist movement that set out to end slavery across this country started in 1688 when German and Dutch Quakers of Mennonite descent made a public protest against slavery in Germantown, Pennsylvania. They published the 1688 Germantown Quaker Petition Against Slavery, which was the first American document of its kind that made a plea for equal human rights for everyone.

The American Revolution started in rural Massachusetts in 1774 when first one town and then another decided that they'd had their fill of unresponsive and unaccountable rule from the British monarchy across a vast ocean, and began to force the King's appointed local judges and council members to resign en masse or face being banished from the places where they lived.

For example, on September 6, 1774, in the town of Worcester, Massachusetts, thousands of militiamen closed the county courts without firing a single shot, making it impossible for the appointed British judges to do their jobs. A month later, on October 4, 1774, the town meeting of Worcester declared that British rule was over and it was time to form a new government, not answerable to the Crown and Parliament. These are the actual moments that launched the American Revolution. The people had finally reached a place in their lived experience of British rule in which they understood that, if government does not serve The People, it is not legitimate and needs to be replaced.

I believe that we are again in a very similar situation to what the people of Massachusetts experienced in 1774. Our government serves the corporations. Our Supreme Court serves the 1%. Therefore, when we find ourselves in an accelerating crisis such as catastrophic climate destabilization, and when we come to understand that our national and state governments are either unwilling or unable to act boldly in the ways that are necessary to respond to this urgency, we have to consider the possibility that it is once again time for We the People to exercise our inherent right of self-government and get on with the task at hand.

We in the community rights movement have already reached that moment of ripeness. We invite you to join us. Our growing collection of towns, cities and counties has declared, under law, that we have the authority to protect our health and welfare, and the rights of our residents (human and otherwise), regardless of whether our state and federal governments are comfortable with our actions. I am proud to be a leading teacher and organizer in this historic movement.

Here's another quote from a previous president of the United States.

> God forbid we should be 20 years without a rebellion. What country can preserve its liberties if the rulers are not warned from time to time that their people preserve the spirit of resistance?

Thomas Jefferson said that in 1787 while he was President! A very gutsy leader!

As I mentioned at the beginning of my talk, what I am proposing tonight is perhaps the most ambitious expansion of community self-government since the American Revolution. **I am proposing a massive program of collaboration between the various climate change protection groups and the community rights movement.** Our goal is the transformation of local community governance across the nation, so that every community is offered the support it would need to participate in this absolutely massive mobilization of communities passing visionary laws that are themselves municipal acts of civil disobedience. For this to become a reality, existing climate change movements would first have to learn a lot more about our rights-based approach, to determine for themselves if this is a direction worth exploring. I am available to participate in those conversations.

As a first step, I will have succeeded in my very ambitious goals this evening if at least ten of you who are active in climate protection groups are ready by the end of my talk to raise your hands and pledge to all of us in this room that you will take the lead in bringing these ideas to your groups, and ideally, become a leading voice in moving this work forward where you live in the months and years to come. I will ask for a show of hands near the end of my talk tonight and request that you leave your full contact info with me at the book table in the back. Start asking yourselves if you might perhaps be one of those ten folks!

And to those of you who are hearing my speech via the nationally syndicated show, Alternative Radio, I am hoping that many of you will also be contacting me soon to find out how you can become a leading voice in the effort to link the climate protection movement and the community rights movement, in order to start passing first dozens and then hundreds and then thousands of local rights-based laws that shift decision-making authority from corporate directors and corporatized politicians to We the People in the local places where we live, so that finally we can all become the leaders we were always meant to be.

The American Revolution was, to a large degree, an anti-corporate-rule revolution.

We may not yet have built sufficient political power to stop entire oil pipelines from being built, or to ban "oil bomb" trains from our nation's tracks or to stop fracking everywhere, but we do already have the capacity to stop these toxic activities where we live in the very immediate future, as I have already described in some of the existing community rights law making. And that's a heck of a good place to start!

We also have some extraordinary revolutionary law and history on our side, to help the public understand that what we are proposing has, in a sense, been done before. Did you know, for example, that the American Revolution was, to a large degree, an anti-corporate-rule revolution? The original 13 colonies were crown corporations, ruled by the British monarchy. Immediately after the revolution, the founders subordinated the newly redesigned business corporation, and defined what it was allowed to do and to be.

Continuing for almost a century, business corporations were prohibited from donating money to candidates or elected officials in government. (In fact, this was still considered a felony in Wisconsin until 1953.) Corporations were also prohibited from donating money to civic and charitable organizations. Corporations did not yet have a recognized voice, a right to speak, which meant that they had no political or commercial speech. Corporate directors and stockholders were held fully liable for all harms and debts. There was no limited liability. Corporations existed at the whim of the state via a limited corporate charter, which could be revoked at any time and for any reason by a state legislature. **Let's remember what has already been accomplished in our nation's history and realize that we don't have to reinvent the wheel, every time we are trying to protect our communities and our world from corporate harm.**

Let's think really big and imagine how we could be using rights-based local law-making to put business corporations back in their histor-

ically subordinate role, which would also give us the boost we need to start phasing out carbon-intensive activities and phasing in renewable energy for much of our needs, such as transportation, food, manufacturing, and more.

Naomi Klein says, "There is no doubt that moving to renewables represents more than just a shift in power sources but also a fundamental shift in power relations between humanity and the natural world on which we depend." That's an important detail to keep in mind as we learn to ask ourselves: what sort of community, what sort of society, do we most deeply long for?

I have taken the liberty of writing up a substantial list of ideas for local ordinance topics. When you go home tonight, you can find a copy of this full list on our website at www.CommunityRights.US/Book. I'm going to share with you a shorter version of it now.

As I share these suggestions, notice the feelings that arise in your body. Are they feelings of excitement? Of trepidation? Do these ideas make you feel more hopeful about the future, or do they scare or overwhelm you? I am asking you to notice how your body reacts because what is required for us to tackle the climate crisis is a very big deal. As we stop waiting for our leaders to lead, and instead imagine ourselves as the leaders we've been waiting for, everyone who is confronted by what is required is going to experience strong feelings and reactions. So, part of our work is to give ourselves and each other the emotional space we need to grieve, or get angry, or feel some fear, or whatever each of us needs, to prepare ourselves for the work ahead.

Here's my abbreviated list of local ordinance ideas:

- Requiring local lending institutions to provide low-interest loans to individuals and companies proposing carbon-neutral developments, and also prohibiting those institutions from lending money to any new fossil fuel development projects;

- Establishing new local gas taxes at the pump, with all money being used to fund rapid expansion of community-based renewable energy projects and public transit;

- Nullifying the local enforceability of global trade treaties that violate the community's right of self-governance or its health and welfare;

- Prohibiting corporations doing business locally from donating to any candidates or elected officials or participating in any way in ballot initiative or referendum campaigns;

- Prohibiting corporations doing business locally from donating to, or partnering with, non-profit and advocacy organizations;

- Prohibiting any further local fossil fuel extraction, pipelines, coal or oil trains and barges through the community;

- Recognizing, honoring, and enforcing Native treaty-protected rights to the local lands and waters;

- Implementing "polluter pays" principles by passing steep carbon taxes for local industry;

- Requiring local grocery stores to reserve a growing percentage of their shelf space for products grown or produced within 500 miles, phased in over five to ten years;

- Raising the level of local taxation for the affluent, and for large corporations doing business locally, and using that money to upgrade and repair crumbling local infrastructure, and to improve local and regional public transit options;

- Establishing the community's locally enforceable right to clean air, water, and soil, the right to a stable climate, and the right to a sustainable energy future;

- Ending all local government subsidies and tax breaks to the fossil fuel industry;

- Recognizing local natural areas as having enforceable rights to exist, flourish and evolve;

- Using eminent domain laws to seize corporate property and place it under local public control whenever the corporate directors refuse to cooperate with the community's objectives;

- In "transition town" communities that have already written an Energy Descent Action Plan, embedding the existing plan into a local ordinance, with annual enforceable deadlines, that brings the community close to 100% renewables within 10 to 20 years;

- Prohibiting any increase in the number of flights passing through the local airport, and establishing a new tax on all local flights, with all money being used to fund new high-speed rail or other low-carbon transportation options;

- Requiring that all containerized products sold in local stores be fully returnable, truly recyclable or compostable, phased in over five to ten years;

- Prohibiting the privatization of local utilities, and if necessary, reversing previous privatizations, to bring decision-making authority back under local public control;

- Establishing local feed-in tariff programs that encourage small non-corporate players to become renewable energy providers, such as farms, local governments, and cooperatives;

- Implementing democratic planning and decision making authority at the neighborhood level;

And last but definitely not least …

- Prohibiting local media from accepting advertising from fossil fuel companies.

The expanded list can be found at www.CommunityRights.US/Book.

I'll bet some of you are feeling pretty skeptical about how realistic it is for us to achieve many of the things on my list. So, I'll take this moment to remind you that 200 communities and counties in nine states have already taken this very courageous plunge into new legal territory and have already begun to take back their authority to define what their communities are going to look like in the future. Yes, it has taken every one of those places a heck of a lot of work to get those laws passed. But **each and every community concluded that they would rather pass laws to protect their health and welfare, laws that are not yet recognized as legal by other branches of government, rather than risk allowing endless new corporate assaults on their communities.**

I have been searching for a more powerful solution to the climate crisis, but I haven't found one. This is the strategy I am committed to. How about you?

Yes, this is bold work, and it starts with a tremendous amount of public education. This is first done internally among those who are committing to doing the teaching and the organizing; and then externally, initially and most effectively as one-on-one conversations with people we already know, and then in house party settings, where people can trust each other enough to really open up and listen to one another.

Yes, this is ultimately paradigm-shifting work as we ask some of the toughest questions that can be asked, such as:

- What would it look like for us to start living as if we really understood that economic growth can no longer continue on this finite planet floating in deep space?

  And …

- How do we put the brakes on, and then rapidly and drastically turn around, to create something that looks a lot less like the Great Depression and a lot more like what Joanna Macy calls the Great Turning?

  And …

- What would it look like for We the People to actually govern ourselves?

The truth is, when We decide that we are ready to implement sweeping changes in our society, it can happen with astonishing speed. In recent years, we've witnessed this on many occasions. Examples include the astonishingly rapid legalizing of gay and lesbian marriage in almost two-thirds of the states, and the astonishingly rapid legalizing of medical and recreational marijuana across the country. So, we know that rapid change is possible, when the culture is ripe for the change to occur. I believe the culture is ripe.

What would it take to build a rights-based movement like this across the country? Well, each state has its own rules about what kinds of law making are allowed at the local level. Here's a very brief introduction.

In about half of the states, the public has the right to propose and directly pass laws at the local and state level through what's called "initiative and referendum," and our movement has won many community rights initiatives through the ballot box in a number of places. Minnesota is one of the states that does not allow its citizens to make law directly through the ballot box, but this could be changed by amending your state constitution. It would require a lot of work over a number of years but it would be well worth the effort.

In addition, about two-thirds of the states are Home Rule states, which means that your local governments are allowed to write their own mini constitutions, which, in principle, should give you more self-governing authority. But if you try to pass any local rights-based laws through your

Home Rule Charter, you will quickly run up against state pre-emption and Dillon's Rule. Minnesota is a Home Rule state, but only allows cities to participate, not towns or counties. Go figure!

This legal mumbo jumbo is actually part of the problem, as it forms a seemingly impenetrable barrier to local self government, which, again, is by design, not by accident. As we have already seen, **the 1% who wrote all of these laws would much prefer that the rest of us are kept as far away from the levers of power as possible. Therefore, the most effective way to claim our authority as the sovereign people, as community majorities, is to refuse to abide by these unjust and illegitimate structures of law that violate our inherent right to govern ourselves.**

In some communities, where the ballot box is not an option, it may require finding allies who are prepared to run for local office pledging to pass these laws. That's what the Community Rights Alliance of Winneshiek County, Iowa, is currently doing. They recently succeeded at electing one of their two candidates for county government. They still need one or two more to make it over the hurdle to pass their ban on frac sand mining as a violation of their right to clean air, water, and soil, and their right to a sustainable energy future.

You won't hear me claiming that this work will be easy. But the wins, when they come, are huge, because our goal is nothing less than to knock down these unjust and illegitimate structures of law. And frankly, nothing less will suffice, given the ecological and social crises that need to be addressed, and soon!

I imagined young people hearing the stories from their elders about how The People stopped waiting for others to lead and started becoming leaders themselves.

Earlier this evening, I announced that I was looking for ten people who are active in climate protection groups to raise their hands and pledge to take the lead in bringing these ideas to their groups, and becoming a leading voice in the effort to bring the climate change movement and the community rights movement together in your community, and to launch a campaign that begins to model local rights-based law making solutions to the climate crisis. This is your moment. If you raise your hand, you are letting me know that you are potentially willing to make a multi-year commitment to this work where you live. Of course, I would also be making an ongoing commitment to work with you to give you the support you will need. Are you out there in the audience?

I would like to close my talk by sharing a vision I had when I was writing my speech this past week, a vision of what the next 50 years (and beyond) might look like if we did our work well in the places that we live.

First, I imagined small towns and big city neighborhoods becoming the places where bold and creative ideas originated, and were then tossed around and shaped and reshaped, ultimately floating in wider and wider spirals until they became common knowledge. Then they were passed into law in dozens of communities, then hundreds of communities, and then finally, thousands of communities.

I imagined how these laws had transformed all of these places. Folks who normally would never have met would find themselves in close working relationships, agreeing about a surprising number of things, especially when they stayed focused on their deepest longings for the kind of community they wanted to create for their children to thrive in.

Then I imagined what might be going on in those communities 50 years from now, when at least some of us here today will still be alive. I imagined young people hearing the stories from their elders about how The People stopped waiting for others to lead and started becoming leaders themselves, and what a huge difference that made in the speed at which we were able to change how we lived and how we produced energy and food and how we moved ourselves from place to place.

That the biggest and most significant change of all, we had come to realize, was learning how to trust ourselves enough to take back our authority to govern ourselves. That once enough of us had awakened to our own power as The People, the rest was almost a piece of cake.

The kids grew up thinking that this was normal, for the adults to directly tackle whatever really big community issues arose. It hadn't felt easy or normal at all for the grown-ups, at least not at first, but they pulled it off, for the most part, with great humility and kindness and patience.

Last, but definitely not least, I imagined that people had started to notice that the giant floods and droughts and hurricanes and wildfires had stopped growing in scale, and people were beginning to celebrate as they started to believe that they were finally experiencing the roughest edge of their badly destabilized climate, which might still continue at this pace for another few generations, but was unlikely to get much worse. People were starting to tell stories to each other about what the world might be like in another 200 years, as the climate finally began to stabilize once again. What an extraordinary period that next 200 years was going to be for everyone who was alive to watch it unfold, as the extreme weather events came less and less frequently.

As we engage in this work, it is critical that we give ourselves a story of that work being successful. We need to believe deep in our hearts that we can indeed turn this crisis around, even if it takes a few hundred years. For it is our deep and abiding love for this beautiful sphere of living earth, and our equally deep and abiding love for the local places where we live, that will ground us and feed us during these very intense years and decades to come.

As Naomi Klein so eloquently states in her book, "If each of us loved our home place enough to defend it, there would be no ecological crisis, no place could ever be written off as a sacrifice zone."

It's time to stand up and say NO to the pipelines. NO to the coal and oil trains. NO to deep water drilling and Arctic drilling. NO to fossil fuel export terminals. NO to fracking and frac sand mining. NO to the Alberta Tar Sands and the Bakken oil fields. NO to the Keystone XL pipeline and the Enbridge pipeline. Not in my backyard. Not in anyone's backyard. NO!

It's also time to stand up and say YES to a steady state zero-growth economy. YES to living in balance with the rest of nature. YES to Indigenous land rights. YES to 100% renewable energy. YES to living in a world that is safe, just, and at peace. We can do this. We must do this. It is time.

Thank you so much.

Protecting the Right of Our Rivers to Exist, Flourish and Evolve by Dismantling Corporate Rule, Watershed by Watershed

This essay is based on an article I wrote for the Institute for Deep Ecology newsletter in the late 1990s which was titled, "Dismantling Corporate Rule: Watershed by Watershed" and which I have continued to update.

Almost every ecological and social disruption our world currently faces stems ultimately from corporate rule. In the face of this overwhelming power, we citizens have become profoundly alienated from our nation's own governance processes. In our hearts and minds, most of us have abandoned the idea of taking our society back from the corporations. Our hopelessness runs deep and wide.

Instead, we envision "alternatives" and try to convince ourselves that it is okay to start over and create entirely new institutions that will serve us better. In essence, by conceding that the corporations have won, we have abandoned our responsibilities as citizens, as We the People, as the sovereign people that we truly are.

If we understood that corporations are, and always have been, brought into legal existence by our state governments, would we continue merely to resist the endless harms they cause, one at a time? Or would we begin again to exercise our sovereign authority over them? If we remembered that we are all Mother Earth protecting herself, and that our authority comes to us with 15 billion years of experience, would we be more ready to take that plunge together into the darkness to reclaim our world?

Corporations have become powerful, not simply by amassing great wealth. Rather, they have done so by means of dozens of Supreme Court decisions, beginning in 1819 and continuing to this day, that illegitimately grant corporations constitutional "rights." The courts now protect, under law, corporations' free speech rights, property rights, right against search and seizure, right of religious freedom, right to a jury trial, right of contract, and on and on.

Imagine for a moment all of us who work tirelessly to protect our world, within a narrow, single-issue framework and in relative isolation, challenging one corporate harm at a time: one timber harvest plan, one endangered species, one toxic spill, one plant closure, one health insurance travesty, one oil pipeline, one threat to our food supply, one manipulated election at a time. Is this really the best we can do? I don't think so!

I am a leader in the fast-growing community rights movement, which, since 1999, has helped more than 200 communities in 12 states to pass legally binding and locally enforceable laws that ...

- strip corporations of their so-called constitutional "rights";

- enshrine the inherent right of the local community to govern itself and to set a higher standard for protecting its own health and welfare, as well as establishing rights for nature locally; and

- ban specific corporate activities which are currently legal under state or federal law, but which the community considers harmful.

We always begin this work at the town or city or county level of governance, and then move our citizen authority upwards from local to state and ultimately to federal laws and constitutional change. But imagine if we could additionally reorient our self governance decision making boundaries to those that are bioregionally designed.

Governance by watershed is not as far-fetched
as you might think.

Many of the communities and counties in our movement have already passed Right to Water and Self-Government ordinances. However, water doesn't respect the straight lines on maps that were devised by conquerors of both the land and the original people who have lived here for thousands of years. Imagine instead if we began to utilize community rights strategies to protect our land and water, based on the actual watersheds that we all inhabit.

Folks in Deschutes County, Oregon, have envisioned what it might look like if they first passed a Right to Water ordinance in their county that protects "the right of the Deschutes River to exist, flourish and evolve." And then followed up on that win with identical county-based ordinances down the watershed, all the way to the river's mouth at the Columbia River. Once the entire Deschutes River watershed had locally enforceable rights to exist, flourish and evolve, those four counties (Deschutes, Jefferson, Wasco and Sherman) could then fundamentally rethink and redesign their governance boundaries in such a way that the residents of the entire Deschutes River watershed could rightfully claim a new form of self-governing authority that could much more effectively defend the rights of the river. Imagine that!

Governance by watershed is not as far-fetched as you might think. The state of California initiated state level water management planning many years ago using watershed boundaries rather than artificial straight lines drawn across landscapes. Here's a brief excerpt from an article titled, "Comparing Complexity in Watershed Governance: The Case of California."

> Watershed-scale management is often touted as a solution to the complexity of water governance. A watershed is defined as the land area that drains to a specific location, often a lake, river confluence, or estuary. The idea of the watershed as an organizing concept for water management has a long history, from river basins acting as functional units in 3rd Century China to John Wesley Powell's proposal that the Western U.S. states should be created around rivers. In more recent years, its popularity has spread, particularly with the advancement of Integrated Water Resource Management in the 1990s. Indeed, Davidson and de Loë called the watershed the "de facto ideal boundary" among water managers and practitioners. The perceived effectiveness of this idea was highlighted in a recent article on Powell's proposal, which argued that Powell's foresight [to create watershed-based states] might have prevented the 1930s dust bowl and perhaps, today's water scarcities.

Across this enormous U.S. landscape, Americans are rapidly coming to terms with the fact that our elected and appointed leaders are leading us off a cliff, and that We are the real leaders we've been waiting for. Would you like to join the conversation about governance by watershed? I'd love to hear from you!

Salmon Coming Home:
A Clayoquot
Restoration Camp

For as long as I can remember, I have been dreaming up wildly ambitious project and campaign ideas. Most of them at least get written down, before my over-active brain and heart move on to other big ideas, such as the proposal to launch an international campaign to end U.S. government and corporate assaults on the world's people and nature. (See that essay, *Enough Already!*, on page 142.)

Rarely do my ideas manifest in actual reality; but on this particular occasion, I woke up one morning in March 1995, in my friend Ian's guest bedroom in Vancouver, British Columbia, and there inside of me lay the entire ambitious sweep, down to the last detail, of a wild and wonderful idea. I would gather allies around me and we would create, on the ground, a summer-long ecological restoration educational pilot project, massive in scale, encompassing the entirety of a steep clearcut on the road to Tofino on the wild west coast of Vancouver Island, Canada, where I was living. The project would be called, "Salmon Coming Home: A Clayoquot Restoration Camp." In 1993, I had played an active role in helping to organize and coordinate Clayoquot Summer, which until 2021 was the largest sustained nonviolent civil disobedience campaign in Canadian history. More than 900 people got arrested blockading logging operations that summer, attempting to stop the destructive logging practices in British Columbia's rapidly disappearing ancient forests. (As of this writing, more than 1100 people have been arrested blockading logging roads in Fairy Creek on Vancouver Island.) Clayoquot Summer was a profound learning experience for me. I had witnessed with my own eyes the mainstream culture of an entire nation shifting awkwardly towards a new recognition of the urgent need to protect these remnant forests. The whole world was watching.

Most people thought we had accomplished miracles. And indeed, logging in Clayoquot Sound was put on hold for quite a while. But what was less obvious at the time was that our summer of actions had profoundly alienated and enraged the local rural communities that depended on logging and milling for their very financial survival. **We at Friends of Clayoquot Sound had naively imagined loggers and millworkers to be our opponents in this struggle, as if their interests were no different than the logging corporation leaders.** I realized, after the fact, that we had lost a golden opportunity to try to figure out how to make alliances with these forest workers, to co-envision an entirely different set of logging policies that would leave the ancient forests standing. So, in 1994, I asked the Friends of Clayoquot Sound Board to make me their labor liaison, and I began an active outreach effort to the forest workers in the nearby village of Ucluelet.

There I was one morning, waking up in Vancouver in March 1995, and into my head and heart popped the idea for another summer-long event in Clayoquot Sound. But this time it would be one that brought environmental protectors and Native people and loggers and mill workers together, to learn the art and skill of large-scale ecological restoration. All of us working side-by-side to begin to heal these badly wounded landscapes so that someday the salmon could actually return here. The goal was for this ambitious event to happen that very summer, so I needed to move fast.

Long story short: My friend and colleague Ernie Yacub joined me as my co-organizer. Many other people offered to volunteer their services, some traveling from as far away as California. We put together a very impressive eight-page printed program which I have reproduced here in the pages that follow. Thousands of copies were distributed across Canada and the U.S. west coast states, to entice large numbers of people to come to the camp and stay for awhile. However, we had failed to remember the most important detail: without significant funding there would be no restoration camp.

In retrospect, we set ourselves up for an obvious disaster. We had a full project ready to launch, but no money to launch it. We did try. We met with a number of potential major donors, but our project was too "far out" for any of them to fund, and foundations needed a much longer time window to consider our proposal. We had given ourselves less than four months from initial conceptualization to opening day at the restoration camp: a huge mistake.

Looking back, I can see clearly that if we had planned the camp for Summer 1996 instead of 1995, it might well have been a smashing success. But we were young and impatient.

Years later, I would still meet folks across Canada who would ask me how the restoration camp had gone, and how sad they were that they had missed such an amazing event! Our printed program, and the tremendous buzz that it generated, had convinced many people that it had indeed taken place as planned!

Here's the message I most want you, the reader, to take away from this story: **It is not too late for your logging-impacted community to organize an event modeled on ours.** This is an eminently organizable concept. I will help you! I mean this from the bottom of my heart! I want to see a large-scale ecological restoration camp somewhere in North America, in the not-too-distant future. Who's ready to make this event a reality?

Please take the time to read through the eight-page program. I guarantee you that it will impress. We had an amazing idea. We just didn't give it sufficient time to become reality. It's not too late! It's yours, if you want it!

salmon coming home

Annie George.

a clayoquot restoration camp

One of the things we all have in common is an interest in seeing Clayoquot Sound's future put on a more ecologically sustainable path which is ultimately managed by the local communities themselves in the context of a just settlement of Native land title. Towards this end, the newly formed Cascadia Restoration Society.....

continued from front page ...
(in partnership with the Friends of Clayoquot Sound) is organizing the first of many restoration and education camps in a highly visible clearcut adjacent to the Alberni/Tofino highway in Tla-o-qui-aht territory (Clayoquot Sound). The Restoration camp has received approval in principle from Tla-o-qui-aht Hereditary Chiefs Ray Seitcher and George Frank, and Chief Councilor Francis Frank. This project provides an opportunity for sectors of the community which have often found themselves in conflict to work side by side. A number of credentialed people will be on site throughout the summer to plan and guide the work, notably Richard Gienger from the Mattole Restoration Council in northern California, one of the oldest large-scale community-based restoration projects in North America.

Until the early seventies, healthy populations of chum and coho salmon spawned in the creek now called Hydro Hill West. An unbroken web of life connected the salmon, the forest, and its many resident creatures, including humans. Clearcut logging and road building destroyed the creek and its tributaries and the salmon no longer have a home, the forest dwellers have little food, and the forest floor has been exposed to pounding rain, summer sun, and fierce coastal winds. Establishing a restoration camp in this small watershed is a manageable first step in a process of reversing the damage that has been done in the cutblocks and in our communities.

Small work groups, led by experienced guides, will tackle a variety of restoration projects in the clearcut. The work activities will be organized in such a way as to ensure that absolutely anyone, young or old, weak or strong, can play a significant role.

Ecological restoration cannot bring back the ancient rainforests. But what we can do is help prevent topsoil from being washed down to Kennedy Lake, thus helping the watershed return to a self-regulating equilibrium. One of the most damaging legacies of clearcut logging is the roads, a leading source of erosion. We will focus our attention on the inactive roads by opening up the drainages which had once crossed the roads unhindered (but are now blocked by clogged culverts or redirected to other drainages for the benefit of the road's design), and planting alder starts there. We may pull boulders and woody debris out of small stream beds, and use this debris to create temporary stream channel walls to protect the drainages. On these constructed walls and some bare slopes, we may again plant fast-growing alder starts so that the walls eventually become living structures once again. In creeks where salmon used to spawn, but which are now filled many feet

deep with tons and tons of rock and woody debris, we will remove some of the debris and/or open the channels. We will give additional attention to the creeks' riparian zones as these areas will have to endure repeated flash flooding for many years until the shallow soils on the steep walls of the watershed are once again held in place by a living mat of wild rainforest.

Salmon Coming Home: a Clayoquot Restoration Camp will have two other primary focusses, each of which offers tremendous and varied volunteer opportunities:

1) **Public Education:** Our highly visible location beside the main highway to Tofino will provide us with ample opportunity to inform and educate visitors and locals. Our front gate kiosk will introduce visitors to the activities on site, provide information that they can take with them, and invite them to participate. They can walk around the clearcut following roads transformed into interpretive trails. Numerous workshops and talks throughout the summer will afford opportunities to examine the issues further (see summer program enclosed).

2) **Forest Watch Trainings:** There are three primary aspects to the Friends of Clayoquot Sound's Forest Watch program:
   • investigating recently logged areas and newly-built roads, searching for transgressions of guidelines and regulations and the terms of cutting and road permits, and reporting transgressions to government.
   • investigating proposed logging areas, searching for inaccuracies in logging plans, such as stream classification, wildlife habitat, terrain stability and visual concerns. Reporting these inaccuracies to government can result in the deferral or cancellation of cutting permits.
   • exposing the destructive reality of on-the-ground logging in the Sound by releasing photographs, videotape and information about recent logging to the media and to other environmental groups.

The Clayoquot Restoration Camp is an opportunity to expand the Forest Watch program in Clayoquot Sound, and to encourage visitors to start such programs in their own communities. Are you interested in becoming a trained Forest Watch volunteer? If your answer is yes, you will be asked to meet the following prerequisities:

a) attend Mark Wareing's evening plus full day Forest Watch introductory course (offered twice a week at the Camp all summer long),

b) attend Mark's evening plus full day follow-up course (offered once a week at the Camp), and...

c) stay at least another three weeks and take an active role in FOCS' forest monitoring field work.

June:

•27th - Camp formally opens for the summer. *(This date has historic significance. It was 90 years ago today that the Industrial Workers of the World [IWW] were founded at a mass convention in Chicago. In a sense, the Convention marked the beginning of working people gaining significant control over their own lives as it was the IWW (the Wobblies) who organized the first trade unions of forest workers and others in North America. They suffered terrible abuse and sometimes even massacres, but in the end succeeded in protecting many of the human rights that some of us now take for granted. The IWW's vision was to create a human society at peace with itself where all were equal, and where local communities had control over their own destinies.)*

July:

•1st @ 1 pm - Official Opening Ceremonies and renaming of the creek. We have invited the Tla-o-qui-aht First Nation to participate.

•8th - "Restoring the Forest Through Holistic Thinking": pm workshop / walkabout & evening slideshow/talk by Ray Travers (Ecoforester).

•9th - an evening talk by Eric Anderson (forestry policy analyst).

•21st - "The critical importance of the labour and environmental movements listening to and learning from each other": an evening talk by Lyle Fenton (Health, Safety and Environment rep for Squamish CAW).

•22nd - "International Law As An Instrument of Social Change": a full-day teach-in led by Joan Russow (U Vic lecturer and activist) and others. $20 to $75 sliding scale donation (all meals included); no one turned away.

•22nd - an evening of eccentric theatre from Antioch U in Ohio.

•23rd - "Community Money, Personal Money, New Money": full-day teach-in led by Michael Linton (LETS System designer). $20 to $75 sliding scale donation (meals included); no one turned away.

•23rd - an evening multilogue on money with Michael Linton (see above).

•26th - "The need for unity between environmentalists and the labour movement": an evening talk by George McKnight (long-time Port Alberni politician and active IWA member for 40 years).

•29th - "Road construction in sensitive areas": a pm walkabout @ Kenquot led by Clive Pemberton (IWA camp chairman for Kennedy Lake Division & an engineer, driller/blaster, roadbuilder).

•29th - "The relationship between the IWA, MB, and the environmental movement": an evening talk by Clive Pemberton (see above).

•early July - "The positive role that unions can and have played in environmental issues, and the very real threat that certain policy changes pose to the livelihoods of union members": an evening talk by Geoff Meggs (editor of Pacific Current magazine, labour journalist of 12 years & author of Salmon).

•late July - "The ecological crisis caused by fishfarming": an evening talk by Alexandra Morton (director of Raincoast Research).

•late July - evening of videos and chat with Mark Achbar (co-director of "Manufacturing Consent").

•late July - "The IWA and its relationship to the logging corporations": an evening talk by Lyn Kistner (former IWA activist).

August:

•8th - "A Citizens Guide to protecting Mother Earth and yourself under an ever-widening ozone hole" - evening talk by Bruce Torrie (Skies Above Foundation-Victoria) & Rhys Roth (Atmosphere Alliance-Olympia, WA).

•9th - "The challenge of maintaining and regrowing the forests under a rapidly changing regime of global temperatures and radiation": a full-day teach-in led by Bruce Torrie, Rhys Roth, and others (see 8th listing). $20 to $75 sliding scale donation (all meals included), no one turned away.

•10th to 13th - Rainforest Action Network Americas-wide Chautaqua at Clayoquot Island. Many presentations at our Camp re rainforest actions across the Americas.

•16th - "Taking on the Corporations" - evening talk shared by Richard Grossman of Provincetown, MA (activist and co-author; Fear at Work: Job Blackmail, Labour & the Environment and Taking Care of Business: Citizenship and the Charter of Incorporation) and Ward Morehouse (president of the Council on International and Public Affairs).

•17th - "The need to protect and rebuild the sovereignty of Nations throughout the world": an evening talk by Lavina White (Hereditary Chief and Matriarch of the Haida Nation).

•18th - "The law in relation to aboriginal rights and the global economy": an evening talk by Bill Lightbown (past BC president of Association of Non-Status Indians, past president of United Native Nations, and an aboriginal activist for 45 years).

•17th-19th - "Rethinking the Corporation/Rethinking the Sovereign Nation": A 3-day workshop intensive co-led by 4 extraordinary social movement leaders: Richard Grossman and Ward Morehouse (see 16th listing), Lavina White (see 17th listing), Bill Lightbown (see 18th listing). $60 to $200 sliding scale donation (all meals included); no one turned away for lack of funds. 40 participants max, pre-registration recommended.

•19th/21st - tentative: Dana Lyons and Jim Page (some of the finest political wordsmithing and great music in our movement) in concert together.

•20th - "Alternative Mythologies" :evening talk by researcher and thinker Joyce Nelson.

•No confirmed date - "The state of the campaign to protect the grizzly": an evening slideshow and talk by Candace Batycki (Grizzly Project).

•No confirmed date -workshop ,talk by Judi Bari (organizer, Redwood Summer & IWW union organizer among California forest workers). see page 7

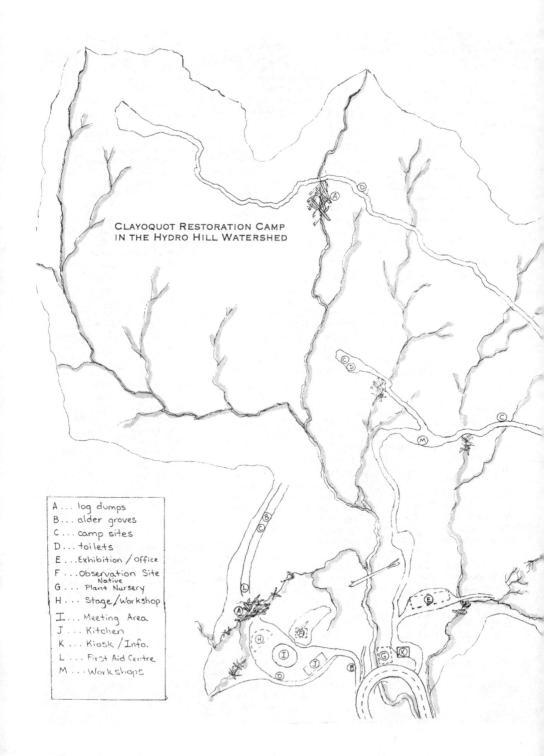

CLAYOQUOT RESTORATION CAMP
IN THE HYDRO HILL WATERSHED

A . . . log dumps
B . . . alder groves
C . . . camp sites
D . . . toilets
E . . . Exhibition / Office
F . . . Observation Site
      Native
G . . . Plant Nursery
H . . . Stage / Workshop
I . . . Meeting Area
J . . . Kitchen
K . . . Kiosk / Info.
L . . . First Aid Centre
M . . . Workshops

Everything You Need to Know to Visit Us This Summer...

Q: Where is the Restoration Camp located?

The Camp is located 67 kilometres west of Port Alberni on Highway 4 off the Vancouver Island Highway. The trip takes about 5 hours from Vancouver, 4 from Victoria and 8 from Seattle. It's just down the hill from Larry Lake in a steep highway-frontage clearcut watershed currently named Hydro Hill West Creek(!). You can't miss it!

Q: Can I drive my car to the Camp and leave it there in a safe location?

No, there will be no available overnight parking at the site. Available parking will be reserved for local day visitors, tourists, people with special needs, and the media. (See next question.)

Q: If the Camp has no overnight parking, how do I get there?!

You take the bus (or hitchhike or bicycle - a grueling ride with lots of traffic and minimal shoulders):

Pacific Coach Lines runs twice daily service from Vancouver's bus station (now at Via Rail Station) to Clayoquot Sound (leaving Vancouver at 8am and noon). And Island Coach Lines makes two runs daily from Victoria to Nanaimo with good connections to busses heading to Clayoquot Sound (leaving Victoria at 805am and 1145am). If originating in Nanaimo, catch the 11am or 3pm bus. All busses stop in Port Alberni; if you need to do shopping there, arrive on an earlier bus. Approximate daily arrival of the bus at the Camp is 140 pm and 6pm. Tell the driver you wish to get off at the bottom of Hydro Hill just before Kennedy Lake. (Certain bus schedules are currently being overhauled - confirm before you travel.)

We intend to provide *additional* daily round-trip bus service from Port Alberni to Ucluelet and Tofino via the Restoration Camp seven days a week. The service is planned to supplement the existing two runs and thus makes it even easier to leave your car at home or in Port Alberni. The schedule and specific terminus point in Port Alberni are not yet confirmed. Please phone us before you travel as this added service is entirely dependent on our raising enough additional funds in the weeks leading up to opening day on June 27th. (Hint Hint)

We are also researching the feasibility of renting a secure parking area in or near Port Alberni where campers could safely leave their cars for a week or a month and be shuttled to the existing bus service. Stay tuned!

Q: Who's invited to participate at the Camp?

Everyone!!!

Q: Can I show up at the Camp without prior notice?

We would prefer that you reserve your place well in advance as soon as you know the approximate dates of your visit. With your help, we can assure a steady population which will ease our cook's job considerably and help us to plan more effectively. On the last page of this paper is a form you can fill out and return to us to let us know your plans.

Q: Will this Camp be like the '93 Peace Camp?

It will be different in a variety of ways:

First, the meals ain't free. The more shifts you work - whether doing restoration work, helping in the kitchen, doing childcare, or leading site tours - the more free meal coupons you'll collect. Non-volunteering campers are welcome for up to five days, and will be asked to pay for their meals.

Second, in order to train as many people as possible in basic ecological restoration skills, we ask that you stay no longer than a month unless you intend to coordinate one of the myriad project groups or join the Forest Watch monitoring.

Third, all campers will be asked to check in upon arrival and sign a Statement of Rights and Responsibilities which they agree to abide by during their stay (as well as a Liability Waiver).

And finally, the Camp will not function as a base for any nonviolent civil disobedience this summer. **see next page**

see next page

Of course, that doesn't mean it isn't going to be a heck of a lot of fun! The summer will be packed with talks, workshops, teach-ins's, performances, and field trips. A healthy mixture of work and play. And again plenty of opportunity to create a strong community feeling.

Q: How will the volunteer work be organized?

There are literally dozens of jobs you can fill once you arrive. You are welcome to stick with one type of volunteer work or learn how to run the whole camp! A summary of these jobs is listed elsewhere in this newspaper.

Q: Are my kids and teens welcome to join me?

Absolutely! We want families to come and work together!

Q: How do my family and friends write or phone me while I'm living at the Camp?

Your family and friends are welcome to send you letters addressed as follows:

Cascadia Restoration Society, Attention:Jane Doe, Box 587, Tofino, BC V0R 2Z0 Canada

Or they may send you letters by fax at 604-725-2527 and addressed as above.

We will do our best to link letters and parcels with their intended receivers but cannot guarantee 100% success as thousands of people may be passing through the Camp over the three month period.

There will be no phone access at the Camp. The nearest public phone is 21 kilometres away. Please leave our new office phone number (604-725-4431) with your loved ones in case of an emergency, but please also let them know that this is <u>not</u> a message phone for campers unless it is truly an emergency.

Q: When was the Hydro Hill West watershed logged and what was it like before?

It was clearcut in 1985/86 by BC Forest Products (since transmogrified into Fletcher Challenge [New Zealand] and now Interfor). Prior to logging, drivers used to note this long sharp curve as the deepest darkest stretch on the entire highway to Tofino. The road was narrow and never got any sun. The Ministry of Forests (MoF) initially replanted the block with cedar and hemlock in 1987 and took it back from the company's Tree Farm License in 1989/90. A planting survey (i.e. spacing, species composition, etc.) was done in 1992 and will be done again this summer. It appears that the clearcut was never herbicided. It is currently in a Small Business category under MoF which intends to upgrade and extend the existing mainline logging road in the summer of 1996 and continue clearcutting to the edge of a small lake at the headwaters of the adjacent watershed.

The watershed has an eventful recent history. It gets its name (rumour has it) because that's where the crew camped out when the Hydro lines were first put in across the island. The creek had already suffered major long-term erosional damage due to the construction of the Hydro lines and original gravel highway. The creek suffered further indignities when an oil tanker truck lost control in the curve of the narrow road, tipped upside down over the creek, and spilled oil all the way to Kennedy Lake. The site has also seen many severe debris torrents which have washed out the highway more than once. When the creek was still healthy, it nurtured coho and chum populations. Remnant anadromous fish populations still survive.

Q: If I can't visit the Camp this summer, are there other ways for me to help?

Yes, lots of ways:

•You can help raise money to offset the costs of the training and food for your friends and neighbours who *are* attending (we estimate about $20 a day).

•You can scan our "Needs List" elsewhere in this paper and help us with the search.

•You can write supportive letters to your local paper and let the BC Government know that you wish to see more public money directed towards community-led restoration projects.

•You can help publicize the Camp in your own community.

•You can ask the organization you are active with to send us an endorsement letter on their letterhead.

•You can ask your local natural foods store and/or supermarket to make a weekly donation to the Camp.

•You can visit our Home Page on the Internet and use the info you find to organize in your community.

On the ground and on the net (Talk to us!):

•*Write us a letter:*
Cascadia Restoration Society
Box 587, Tofino, BC V0R 2Z0 CANADA
•*Phone us:* (604) 725-4431 •*Fax us:* (604) 725-2527
•*Email us:*
yacinfo@mars.ark.com (Ernie Yacub), *or*
focs@web.apc.org (c/o 'Paul', 'Linda' or 'Joanna')
•*Visit us in cyberspace:*
keep in touch with the latest developments at the camp, send us email, and retrieve files of useful information. This is brand new, so it will take us a little while to get the system & information exchange operating smoothly.
World Wide Web:
http://www.alternatives.com/groups/restore/index.html
Telnet: alternatives.com (204.244.17.10)
go to organizations in top menu. BBS: 604-430-8080
•*Production Team for this newsmagazine:*
Paul Cienfuegos, Ernie Yacub, Jan Brubacher, Joanna Gislason, Annie George, Linda Mimeault, and Derek Smith. Thanks to Matthew Pollock, Michael Linton, Phil Mayhew, and Dauphin St Amant.

6 ∞ salmon coming home

September:

- 2nd to 4th - A reunion of all the Clayoquot arrestees from throughout the years. Come join us for the long weekend and share your memories. The weekend kicks off Saturday with an evening of stories and reflections, led by Olga Schwartzkopf and Peter Light, about the '93 arrests and trials.

- 5th - "Forest Policy in BC: A History of Corruption": an evening talk by Matthew Pollock (forest policy analyst).

- 8th - an evening with author broadcaster humourist Des Kennedy.

- 12th to 16th - Society for Ecological Restoration (SER) annual conference in Seattle. Paul Cienfuegos presenting a paper on the Camp.

- 18th - "Restoration as a way of life": an evening of theatre, comedy, and other stuff with Freeman House (bioregionalist, writer and watershed organizer) and David Simpson (founder of the Mattole Watershed Salmon Support Group and author/playwright of "Queen Salmon").

- 19th - "Watersheds as a Unit of Perception": full-day workshop co-facilitated by Freeman House & David Simpson (Mattole Restoration Council). $20 - $75 sliding scale donation (meals included); no one turned away.

- 19th?? - "Beyond Hope - The Business Route", evening one-hour, two-animal play, written and performed by Doug Gook and his horse, fresh from Vancouver Fringe Festival: "through the appreciation and respect for shit

and piss, these two weave a rant of rural and urban interplay, horse logging, and institutional/corporate excess". $5 to $15 sliding scale donation; no one turned away.

- 21st/22nd - 2-day workshop in sacred ritual, one outcome of which will be the planning and facilitation of Autumnal Equinox Festival on the 23rd. $40 to $150 sliding scale dona-tion (all meals included); no one turned away. Pre-registration recommended.

- 23rd - Full day Autumnal Equinox Festival and Closing Celebration.

- 24th - International Rivers Day: surprise event planned.

- 25th - Camp formally closes. Thanks so much for joining us!!!

Ongoing:

- periodic talks and presentations by a variety of Nuu-chah-nulth community members on a wide variety of subjects including Native land title, updates on current treaty negotiations, Native history and struggle with colonial systems, traditional uses of native plants, salmon stories, etc.

- Mark Wareing RPF will be living at the camp 3 weeks out of every 4 all summer long beginning July 9th, and leading 3 full-day Forest Watch/Forest Ecology workshops each week.

- weekly talks by trade union activists all summer.

- periodic talks by Hereditary Native leaders from throughout BC.

- periodic workshops with Kevin Pegg on alternative energy sources and technologies.

- Valerie Langer's famous clearcut and tree-farm tours two days each week.

Dear friends and allies -

We need your active support and involvement to succeed. Can you help us with one or more of the following tasks? - fundraising, publicity and promotion, local organizing, camp infrastructure, etc. Please begin by returning the survey form below and on reverse. And thanks in advance for your assistance!

__ Please add me to your mailing list. I enclose at least $10 towards expenses.

__ Please accept my donation of $_____:
  (Make your cheque payable to Cascadia Restoration Society. If you're Canadian and require a tax receipt, please make it payable to FOCS-CRS.)

__ I can help with fundraising. Please contact me for further information.

__ I plan to attend the Camp. Details on reverse.

__ I have friends or associates who may be able/willing to make a significant donation (financial, in-kind, or human labour) to your project. I enclose details.

__ I would like to offer/organize a workshop, talk, training or performance. I enclose details of my offer.

__ I know of important books, journals or other items which I can help you obtain for your Camp's sales kiosk.

__ I will organize an evening in my community for you to publicize the Clayoquot Restoration Camp.

__ Please send a copy of this publication to the names/addresses/faxes/emails I have listed.

Name_____ Phone/Fax_____ _____ Email_____

Address_____

Volunteer opportunities galore at the Camp:

The Camp offers limitless volunteer opportunities. Besides restoration work and trail-building, we need your help in one or more of the following:

Camp construction, maintenance and support: construction of the various buildings and other infrastructure; working in Camp kitchen; childcare; driving our shuttle-busses (class 4 license required); facilitating various group meetings; mediation support for conflict resolution; maintaining the recycling program; maintaining the site's numerous composting toilets; traffic calming outside the main gate and maintaining safe car and pedestrian flow; first aid and emergency preparedness; 24-hour front gate security; office support at our 3 offices (Camp, Port Alberni, Tofino): answering phones, responding to informational requests; computer work, etc.

Education: guiding tourists and media around the Camp; leading workshops in your particular area of expertise; welcoming visitors at front gate - whether orienting new arrivals or answering tourists' questions; behind-the-counter work at our front-gate info and sales kiosk; writing, designing, building, installing, and maintaining of dozens of interpretive display signs throughout the clearcut; articulate guides for Exhibition Tent; writing, designing, building, installing, and maintaining of numerous highway signs; designing, editing and production of Camp brochures, press kits and releases, posters, etc; fundraising in your own communities.

Donations We Are Yearning For

- fax machines (2)
- computers
- modems
- Mac hard drive
- answering machine
- 8 passenger van & car
- small bus we can borrow or rent for the summer
- ATV four-wheeler for hauling supplies on site
- food
- office supplies
- building materials especially fabric like rip-stop nylon & canvas
- lumber
- slide projector
- screen
- cameras
- film
- audio & video tapes
- flash-lights
- display boards
- bulletin boards
- VCR
- TV

Salmon Coming Home: a Clayoquot Restoration Camp is launching a powerful new way to fund grassroots work through "Restoration Dollars", a local money system of merchant credits. In collaboration with Landsman Community Services, designers of Local Exchange Trading System (LETS), we plan to introduce the Restoration Dollar this summer, backed by Victoria businesses.

Introducing the Restoration Dollar!

When you buy Restoration Dollars from Salmon Coming Home, your cash goes to support the project, and in exchange you get an equal number of Restoration Dollars to spend, dollar for dollar, at the participating merchants.

So now you can give generously and spend wisely. Local business people can support good works in the community, and in turn you get to support them with your business. And the Camp gets the long-term funding it needs.

The more people who use Restoration Dollars, the better it will work. You can help by telling us what businesses we should sign up.

Although the first merchant credit system will be located in Victoria (with Nanaimo as a probable second location), the programme can work in any community and can support many other local projects. Let us know if you would like to help develop one in your community. There is a place on the return form below to request further Restoration Dollars information:

$ $

Yes, it's true, we need lots of money to make Salmon Coming Home the transformative event in the struggle for forest protection in Clayoquot Sound. I am enclosing the form below with my contribution.

$ $

__ Please send me more info on 'Restoration Dollars' so I can share it with my friends and relations.

__ I want to interest my local merchants in 'Restoration Dollars'. Send me more info on commercial participation.

__ I wish to distribute Camp materials in my community. I enclose details.

__ I will act as a Contact Person for the Camp and promote the event in my community.

__ I wish to pre-order a copy/ies of the Clayoquot Restoration Sourcebook to be published Sep 95. I enclose $10/copy.

__ I will help with electronic communications (please contact: yacinfo@mars.ark.com).

__ I do not plan to attend the Camp but wish to volunteer from home. What I can offer you is:

__ I plan to attend the Camp as a volunteer. Let me tell you about myself, my interests/skills/experience, and which volunteer tasks most interest me (see listing on inside page):

I enclose details of my time availability (starting now):

__ from today to June 17 - lots of pre-Camp work to do.

__ the week of June 18 to 26 when the infrastructure set-up crew will move on to the site (lots of help needed including construction of temporary structures, food prep, errands galore, site documentation, etc).

__ for the duration of the Camp (June 27 to Sep 25) - please specify dates - one month max: _____

__ the week beginning September 26 when the infrastructure break-down and clean-up work begins.

What physical shape are you in? Can you put in full days of sustained physical work?

Please mail or fax this form to us today. Your speedy response is crucial for the success of the project. Thanks so much!!!

(Cascadia Restoration Society, Box 587, Tofino, BC V0R 2Z0 Canada. Fax 604-725-2527.)

The Democratic
Logging Vision
in Five Acts

What follows is a batch of five stories entitled The Democratic Logging Vision in Five Acts, as all of these pieces are intimately tied together around the urgency of forest protection across the world.

The first two stories frame the mass-extinction-level historical crisis we are now facing on Earth, and some first steps that we must take immediately to turn this ship around.

The final three documents are directly related to The Democratic Logging Project, which I conceptualized in 2002.

I lived in Humboldt County, California from 1995 to 2011. For most of that period, I closely followed the outrageously unethical and illegal activities of Charles Hurwitz and his Maxxam Corporation, which in 1985 had exercised a hostile takeover of the local Pacific Lumber Company, a family-run logging operation founded in 1863. Hurwitz ran the company into the ground, and filed for bankruptcy protection in 2007.

I was peripherally involved for many years in the local movements to protect these ancient redwood forests. Ultimately, I decided that my best contribution was to launch a new paradigm campaign to challenge Maxxam Corporation's decision-making authority (as a corporate "person") over logging policy in Humboldt County, because it became clear to me that fighting one ruinous Timber Harvest Plan (THP) at a time was ultimately a dead end strategy. I invited a diversity of folks from across the county to join me, and we initiated The Democratic Logging Project in 2002.

First, is the draft statement of our groundbreaking project's goals and strategies. Second, the "Dear Neighbor Letter" that we drafted as something we would distribute county-wide. We did not generate a sufficient level of interest or excitement for this paradigm-shifting proposal to move forward and the project never officially launched, but it nonetheless engendered more than a year's worth of very provocative discussions across the county in 2002/2003.

A third document is a letter to the editor that I wrote for the Times-Standard, Humboldt County's corporate daily newspaper, which they refused to publish.

CLEARCUTS AND LANDSLIDES: WHO BENEFITS AND WHO PAYS?

This essay was originally published in Access Journal in July, 1997.

If another nation had done this to our lands, we would call it an act of war.

Let us cut, the industry says, but don't hold us responsible for our logging. We want your trees, but you pay for the logging roads, you fight the fires, you subsidize the sales with your taxes. We want to clearcut steep slopes, but when they slide and bury public roads, you pay for the clean-up and repair. We want to log your watersheds, but when cities cannot use their water supplies because of siltation from our logging, that's just tough. We foul your streams and rivers, and if you have to spend hundreds of millions of dollars to build a water filtration system, that's your problem. If your homes flood, if your insurance rates go up, if you have the misfortune of being killed by a mudslide, hey, that's just too bad. We want to suspend the laws because they're in our way. We want the last old growth. We want the last redwoods. We want. We want.

– Both quotes are from Tim Hermach, Executive Director, Native Forest Council

Throughout the Pacific Northwest and Northern California last fall and winter, thousands of logging-related slides killed at least eight people, buried roads and damaged homes, destroyed countless salmon spawning streams, contaminated public water supplies, crippled agricultural production, and caused general havoc.

According to Andy Stahl, Executive Director of Forest Service Employees for Environmental Ethics (FSEEE), "Political and economic forces created these slides, not God or Nature."

Government and corporate officials continue to try to pass the buck, claiming that more studies are needed to determine if there is indeed a direct correlation between clearcutting and landslides. However, **there is irrefutable evidence, documented over thousands of years of human history, linking logging, flooding and landslides.** Here are three examples:

- Cyprus, 1200 BC: By this date, the effects of deforestation were already well known. Cypriots, having cut the forested slopes, suffered from increased flooding and mudslides. So much mud accumulated in the Hala Sultan Tekke Harbor that it became sealed off from the sea and could no longer be used as a port.

- The Alps, 1618: After felling the forests above the town of Plurs, the earth roared down and buried the town under 70 feet of mud. Not one of its 2430 inhabitants survived. In 1806, 450 people in Goldau lost their lives in a similar incident.

- Dhaka, Bangladesh, October 1988: Originally forested, the now barren slopes of the Himalayas were pounded by rains, causing massive mud torrents which killed 2000 people and left 25 million homeless.

Many recent studies offer further evidence. The U.S. Forest Service did a study after the 1964 storms which found that the greatest soil loss was from mudflows and landslides, and these occurred more frequently at roads and clearcuts. An Oregon State University master's thesis reported that "Landslides occur 24 and 253 times more frequently (relative to forested rate) in clearcuts and road areas, respectively." The Oregon Department of Forestry published in 1995 a document titled, "Cumulative Effects of Forest Practices in Oregon" which found that "Clearcut harvest and/or slash burning on steep slopes may increase failure rates from two to 40 times over rates on undisturbed sites."

Many municipal leaders are already experts on this subject. For example, city officials in Portland and Salem, Oregon have begged that their watersheds not be logged anymore due to economically devastating sedimentation from logging operations.

How large was the toll to human life last winter? It was immense. Near Roseburg, Oregon, four neighbors died when one of their houses was hit by a torrent of boulders, logging slash, uprooted trees and mud from a nine-year-old clearcut on an 80% slope. Said a survivor, "That home exploded, like a bomb had gone off."

Three motorists were knocked off Oregon Hwy 38 by a muddy avalanche. One of them died. A woman and her two children drowned when their car was hit by a tractor-trailer trying to avoid a slide. In the town of Myrtle Creek, Oregon, five homes were knocked off their foundations when a clearcut gave way, shifting tons of wet earth.

In Stafford in Humboldt County, California, seven homes were obliterated and seven more damaged by a mile-long, 100-yard-wide mudslide. The culprit, Maxxam Corporation, has offered to buy the homeowners' properties for $3 million. Eight of the 13 families who lived on the street have since moved away. The callousness of official government and corporate responses has been instructive.

- Says an area director of the Oregon Department of Forestry, "The jury is still out on the issue" of clearcuts and landslides. "The Oregon Department of Forestry is not in the business of protecting houses."

- Only a mile down the road from one of the fatal Oregon slides, Roseburg Forest Products plans to log a similar site, totally ignoring the pleas and concerns of seven homeowners who live directly below the planned logging site.

- West Coast Land and Timber Company (of Coos Bay) is urging forestland owners to ignore a request from the state Forestry Department, asking loggers to voluntarily stop clearcutting on slide-prone slopes above highways and homes.

- Oregon Senator Bill Fisher (R-Roseburg) suggests that the homeowners "were at fault for building their home[s] in the wrong spot." He adds, "Clearcutting is a practice that enables a diverse ecosystem to thrive."

The expense to taxpayers is record-breaking and continues to rise. The early January floods were easily the most expensive in California history, totaling over $1.8 billion. Nearly 300 square miles of northern California were flooded (including the Central Valley's Sacramento River), damaging or destroying 21,000 homes, 3000 mobile homes, and 1900 businesses. At the height of the emergency, 120,000 people had been evacuated. **The cumulative cost, both via taxes and personal loss, is absolutely staggering, and a significant portion of it can be considered another donation by We the People to logging corporations which are not required to pay for the damage they create (i.e. corporate welfare).** To put it in perspective on the local level, here are a few examples:

- Humboldt County: $16.4 million in damage and climbing.

- The lower Klamath River: 28 businesses and more than 50 homes damaged or destroyed, $800,000 just to repair one section of river-bank.

- Forest Service road repair expenses: Siskiyou National Forest (NF) $10 million, Rogue River NF $8 million, Curry County $2 million (and all as quickly as possible so the U.S. Forest Service can reopen the roads in order to sell more healthy ancient groves this summer).

- Jackson County: More than $50 million in damages, including 1200 affected homes.

Not to mention the thousands of individuals who have filed for unemployment assistance after being put out of work by the flooding. The list goes on and on and on.

> *How many more 100-year floods will we citizens*
> *accept before we stop battling one clearcut at a time?*

Will states, counties and municipalities have to raise taxes to cover these expenses? Federal Emergency Management Agency (FEMA) money (i.e., federal taxes) and insurance will pay for much of it. Insurance customers (that is, most of us) will pay for it in increased premiums. There are indications that the insurance industry is seriously overextended and will require a taxpayer bailout.

A better solution? Our governments need to find the courage to send these bills to the real culprits: the logging and other resource extraction corporations.

How many more 100-year floods will we citizens accept before we stop battling one clearcut at a time? Is it enough simply to sue specific corporations for specific harms, or has the time arrived for a new kind of citizen activism, which fundamentally challenges the rights of giant corporations to rule over us? What if we got organized enough, through citizen initiatives or other processes, to ban all corporate involvement in the political process? Would our elected officials continue to ignore majority citizen opinion if they no longer received funds from corporations, if corporate lobbying was banned? This is not a pipe dream. It was the norm in most states throughout the 1800s and remained the law in Wisconsin until 1953.

For more than 100 years, American citizens understood that a corporation was an artificial, subordinate entity with no inherent rights of its own; both law and culture reflected this relationship between sovereign people and the institutions they created. Toward the end of the 19th century, corporations set out to transform the law and recreate themselves as "corporate persons" with constitutional protection. Citizens in massive numbers rose up and organized, educated, and resisted with great passion and energy but lost the battle. By the beginning of the 20th century, corporations had become "sovereign" and in turn had defined We the People as merely consumers, workers, taxpayers, etc. **Today, our law and culture concede our sovereignty to corporations, as do most of our advocacy organizations.**

"But we don't study who We the People are … how sovereign people should act" says Richard Grossman, co-director of the Program on Corporations, Law and Democracy. "We need to realize what power and authority we possess; and how we can use it to define the nature of corporations, so that we don't have to mobilize around each and every corporate decision that affects our communities, our lives, the planet."

Key Resources

- *Man and Nature,* George Perkins Marsh, first published in 1864

- *Railroads and Clearcuts: Legacy of Congress' 1864 Northern Pacific Railroad Land Grant,* Derrick Jensen and George Draffan

- *Landslides and Clearcuts: What Does the Science Really Say?* Doug Heiken

- *Corporate Power, Corruption and the Destruction of the World's Forests*, the Environmental Investigation Agency, Vinciane Bohan

WHY FOREST WORKERS AND ENVIRONMENTALISTS ARE NATURAL ALLIES

This essay was originally published in Access Journal in August, 1997. Sadly, the urgency of its message has not lessened at all since then.

Environmentalists need to confront their class biases ... The environmental movement arises from the cities, the more privileged people, and from the gentrification class of the rural areas ... Once we confront our class biases ... we need to reach to their [the workers] issues ... not as a ruse to get to them, but with the understanding that the way the corporations treat the workers is the same way they treat the forests.

– Judi Bari, forest protector and IWW labor organizer

[T]he export of unprocessed logs, the relentless drive for ever higher levels of automation, the stress on clearcutting as opposed to "new forestry," the use of chemical weed killers, the burning of slash, and so on, make no sense from a worker's standpoint.

– John Bellamy Foster, author of The Limits of Environmentalism Without Class, 1993

I used to live on Vancouver Island in British Columbia and served for a year as the Labor Liaison for Friends of Clayoquot Sound, a tiny village-based organization which did the impossible: orchestrated an international media and nonviolent civil disobedience campaign which virtually halted Mac-Millan-Bloedel Corporation's clearcutting and road building in the ancient local rainforests. For four months during the summer of 1993, 13,000 people of all ages, races, and nationalities visited our base camp, and 900 of them blockaded a logging road deep in the rainforest. It was the largest civil disobedience action in Canadian history (until 2021 at Fairy Creek in British Columbia, where more than 1100 people have thus far been arrested trying to stop the clearcut logging of some of the last 2.5% of ancient forests remaining in Canada).

We thought we were winning, but we were quite mistaken. The biggest reason, in my opinion, is that we failed to understand that the hundreds of forest workers who we were blockading could be our allies and not our enemy. The result? Inter-community tension that you could cut with a knife. Regular death threats of our leading activists. Ultimately, a potentially permanent loss in our ability to ever co-organize around our common ground.

Why couldn't we see it coming? I believe the main reason is that our movement was blind to the class privilege which informed our work. **We simply could not fathom that loggers might also have a strong desire to protect the forests, so as to ensure themselves and their children a secure forest job base well into the future.** In addition, we could not distinguish between the corporation and the workforce. We perceived them as having the same values: cutting the forest down in order to get rich.

By the time I proposed that perhaps loggers were actually our allies, and that we needed, at a minimum, a new staff position to focus on building these relationships, it was too late. The damage had already been done. All chances of real dialogue had evaporated.

It is now 1997. The battle over the future of the ancient forests continues to escalate. As nature's healthy edges recede by the day, the stakes grow higher. Whose on what side? Who are our allies in the campaign? Who are our opponents? **Who the heck are "we" anyway? Are professional D.C. based enviro-lobbyists any more "we" than local loggers worried about their future employment prospects? I'm not so sure.**

Our society is so culturally fractured, and so many of us are now committed to single issue campaigns, that it's almost impossible to gauge how broad-based a movement we could actually build to protect what is left of the ancient forests and the human cultures which depend on them. Most of us don't know our neighbors. Most of us are too timid to share our deep thoughts with our co-workers for fear of alienating ourselves if they think differently than we do. Environmentalists still don't talk to mill workers or loggers. The wealthy don't talk to the unemployed. Euro-Americans rarely have meaningful conversations with Native people or other people of color.

Yet so many in our society are suffering, most of them unorganized and silent. It's a very difficult time in North America for those of us who envision a healthy and equitable society. What is to be done?

I, for one, am ready to commit to doing the hard and challenging work necessary to avoid making the same mistakes that environmental activists continue to make all over the world. What would such a task look like? How would we begin? How would it be organized and sustained for the long-term?

After 20 years of community organizing experience, I think I know some of the answers. Some are more obvious than others. We all need to make it more of a priority to build those personal relationships with people who are "the other." Only after authentic relationships are established can we get down to examining where the common ground lies, and building those relationships is tough! It requires that each of us be willing to really look at the cultural conditioning we carry in our body armor be it, "workers are greedy and don't care about the forest" or "environmentalists are dirty lazy hippies," etc. And that's just the crud at the surface. Below that layer, it gets way more complicated: classism, racism, sexism and more.

In my opinion, here's the hardest piece each group will have to tackle:

Urban environmentalists will finally have to confront and acknowledge the vast amount of class privilege which they are mostly unaware of carrying. They will have to educate themselves about the proud history of working class culture, so that they finally begin to understand that they too are "workers." Then they will no longer blame workers for the sins caused by CEOs in distant corporate boardrooms, and see that most of the freedoms and privileges they take for granted came through workers' social movement struggles. In fact, if unions weren't around, practically all of the wealth would be held by just a few people and the rest of us would be serfs!

Forest and mill workers will finally have to confront their lack of understanding of ecological principles. Ancient forests are not a renewable resource. Protecting biological diversity is essential if nature's species (including humans) are to survive. Our society's standard of living is way beyond the earth's capacity to support us (this includes the lifestyles of most well-paid workers). Perhaps most critically, there must be an understanding that we are all connected in a great web of life, and what we do to the forest has direct impact on all of us.

Forest and mill workers tend to see environmentalists as more of a threat to their jobs than the giant corporations which employ them. Although clearly absurd, it is no accident. Corporations, under the tutelage of public relations fixers, have learned it is easier to have workers fighting their environmental battles for them. Obviously, environmentalists didn't cause the forest crisis, decades of over-cutting and road building did. Environmentalists are simply the messengers with a very unpleasant message.

Unfortunately, environmentalists have their own tunnel vision. They continue to perceive forest and mill workers as uncaring about the natural environment, and interchangeable in their values with the corporations which employ them. This is equally absurd. The fact is, if loggers had the power to set forest policy in the woods, they certainly would not support clearcutting because they would have the longterm interests of their own families and multi-generational communities as their priority.

Loggers don't stand up publicly and oppose clearcutting for obvious reasons: they are pawns in the operation and easily replaced in a society where the government chooses to maintain a high unemployment rate in order to keep workers docile and scared. Forest workers are terrified for their futures and it is simply made worse by an environmental movement which utterly fails to communicate with them in ways which speak to their current fears and anxieties.

To me, there is only one critical division line in our struggle. It's the line between giant corporations and the folks who care about the health of their own communities (and I mean health in the broadest sense: economic, ecological, social, etc).

Imagine a day in the near future when loggers recognize a forest road blockade action for what it is: the activist equivalent of a union picket line, and thus, in a show of solidarity, choose not to cross it because they understand that both groups, activists and loggers, share common ground. Now imagine a larger leap, where both groups are well organized and supported by substantial enough numbers of active and empowered citizens that we no longer have to meet on opposite sides of a blockade because we have become powerful enough to dismantle the corporations which interfere in the lives of our communities. And in their place, we have created locally owned and democratically managed companies.

You may see the picture I paint as impossible pie-in-the-sky fantasy. Perhaps. But the alternative is an increasingly impoverished society, both economically and ecologically, where citizens fight for the crumbs and giant corporations control everything. From my perspective, we have nothing to lose, and a healthy and more equitable world to gain. Are you ready to get off the couch?

I would like to close this essay with a brief excerpt from the "Resolution on Superfund For Workers" adopted in 1991 at the annual convention of the Oil, Chemical and Atomic Workers International Union.

> "WHEREAS, the clash between our productive capacities and the tolerance of nature is heightening each day because our prosperity is based on toxic substances and by-products that cause significant harm to working people, their communities and the environment as a whole; and
> WHEREAS, many workers see the growing environmental clashes and feel angry and frustrated because although they may hold deep pro-environmentalist convictions, they are also not inclined to commit economic suicide; and ..."

Key resources on labor struggles and community organizing

- *A People's History of the U.S.*, Howard Zinn
- *Working: People Talk About What They Do All Day and How They Feel About What They Do*, Studs Terkel
- *When Workers Decide: Workplace Democracy Takes Root in North America*, edited by Len Krimmerman
- *The History of the American Labor Movement*, Philip Foner
- *Rank and File: Personal Histories by Working-Class Organizers*, Alice and Staughton Lynd

Key resources on ecological literacy

- *Ecological Literacy*, David Orr
- *Forest Farmer's Handbook*, Orville Camp
- *Beyond the Limits: Confronting Global Collapse, Envisioning a Sustainable Future*, Donella Meadows

Key resources on building alliances between workers and environmentalists
- *Fear at Work: Job Blackmail, Labor and the Environment,* Richard Kazis and Richard Grossman
- *Timber Wars,* Judi Bari
- *Building Bridges: The Emerging Grassroots Coalition of Labor and Community,* edited by Jeremy Brecher and Tim Costello

TOWARDS A COUNTY-WIDE UPRISING OF CITIZENS ASSERTING OUR AUTHORITY TO GOVERN OURSELVES BY WRESTING CONTROL OF LAND USE DECISION MAKING AWAY FROM MAXXAM CORPORATION AND PUTTING IT IN THE HANDS OF THE PEOPLE WHERE IT RIGHTFULLY BELONGS

Our goals for this campaign are twofold:
- To remove Maxxam Corporation from all of its holdings in the county. We would arrange for its directors to hand over or sell all holdings to a worker and community-controlled new business or nonprofit institution. This new enterprise would focus its energies on seeking to employ local timber industry workers while maintaining appropriate levels of eco-forestry. It would also provide employment through restoring the health of the forest lands.

- To build a democratic movement in Humboldt County that sees itself as part of the national movement to reclaim our sovereignty and democracy from large corporations who effectively rule the United States at this time.

The strategies we plan to use to achieve these goals are:

- We are forming and developing a steering committee to coordinate the campaign. This group will reflect the diverse interests and cultures of the county. Steering committee members will be required to attend a full-day orientation session to help them to understand the new framework, language, and strategy of the campaign. Members will be asked to commit at least five hours/week to the campaign *or* will be asked to commit a significant amount of time on a weekly basis for a minimum of one year.

First Steps for the Steering Committee (immediate undertakings):

- To create an affordable and easily available reading packet to help county residents understand the campaign, and which all new members would be asked to read. This packet will include:

  - a cover letter from the steering committee

  - a description of this campaign

  - background history of corporate power in the U.S.

  - an outline of our legal rights as the sovereign people of the United States of America

  - a list of written resources (books, pamphlets, articles) relevant to this campaign

  - an explanation of why this campaign is specifically operating outside of, and ignoring the regulatory arena

  - an explanation of how this campaign is part of a democratic movement around the country to reclaim our sovereignty over the corporation as an institution.

- To better understand and articulate how Maxxam's corporate personhood and other so-called constitutional "rights" undermine the rights of private property owners, timber industry workers, ranchers and farmers, local business owners, and environmentalists.

- To encourage additional people and groups to join the campaign. All new members would be encouraged to attend a full-day orientation session to help them to understand the new framework, language, and strategy of the campaign.

Mid-term undertakings:

- To launch an alliance of local Humboldt groups intent on stopping Maxxam Corporation's continuing assault on the communities, jobs, watersheds, and democratic institutions of Humboldt County.

- To expand, strengthen and develop our steering committee by reaching out and building working relationships and alliances with diverse groups such as timber industry workers, labor unions, faith-based groups, ranchers and farmers, and environmental organizations.

- To launch a major educational campaign countywide to help local residents to:
  1) learn to distinguish between the legitimate rights of human persons (protected by the Bill of Rights) and the illegitimate "rights" of corporate institutions currently interpreted as "persons" under law.
  2) learn how a democratic local citizens' movement to remove Maxxam Corporation's legal personhood status would provide for much more local control over land use decisions. This would also provide stable job opportunities for timber industry workers.
  3) see themselves as the sovereign people in a democratic republic with the knowledge to act accordingly.

- To reframe the debate about Maxxam Corporation from one which is defined by timber corporation executives (i.e. jobs vs. environment) to one which is defined by the people of Humboldt County. The issue is essentially that the people of our county should be in charge of decisions about local land use, not the leaders of giant absentee timber corporations.

- To call attention to the ways Maxxam Corporation is violating the First Amendment rights of local citizens to speak and assemble:
  1) by prohibiting its employees from publicly stating their concerns about current logging practices, or the closing of mills, for fear of being fired.
  2) by filing a SLAPP (Strategic Lawsuit Against Public Participation) lawsuit against those who are attempting to organize against corporate harms in their communities. SLAPP is designed not to

win in court, but to render opposition ineffective by tying up people's time, energy, and resources and by creating fear of speaking out.

- To name and hold accountable the key decision makers and spokespeople of Maxxam Corporation and our government officials who are providing political cover to the corporation and its crimes against the county.

Longer term undertakings:

- To remove from Maxxam Corporation its ability to utilize various "rights" it claims to possess. The corporation's personhood status would be withdrawn by means of a popular referendum for the county.

- To ultimately pass one or more county ballot initiatives and run and elect candidates which will formally implement these changes in the local culture.

- To prepare the groundwork for a statewide ballot initiative. This would aim to withdraw the personhood status and all other so-called constitutional "rights" from all corporations chartered or doing business in California.

DEAR NEIGHBOR LETTER

The Democratic Logging Project drafted this Dear Neighbor letter in Spring, 2002 as something that we would widely distribute across Humboldt County, California as an initial outreach tool for our project. It was never distributed.

We are writing to you because we believe you would likely share our concerns about some of the things that have happened in our county over the past decades. Jobs have been lost, our economy has been depressed, our children's future has been compromised, our natural resources have been plundered, and our environment has been degraded. All this has taken place over a long period of time and has been caused by the activities of Charles Hurwitz and his Maxxam Corporation. It has culminated in the devastation that we have all witnessed; this is a force in our midst that is dividing us.

Many of us in this county have felt the repercussions of the theft of Pacific Lumber by Hurwitz. Whether it is the loss of our jobs, the flooding of our property, or the degrading of our water, a great deal of the damage done to this community can be traced back to the people in charge of Maxxam Corporation.

We wanted to know how this could happen. The story of our county is similar to the story of many communities across the United States, where people are increasingly the victims of a boom and bust economy. We still found ourselves asking why this happens. And why can't we do anything about it? How can one corporation, such as Maxxam, wield so much power that it brings an entire community to its knees? **Why is Maxxam Corporation's "right" to make a profit greater than our personal and property rights, as well as our collective rights as a community?** What of our right to a decent livelihood? Or our right to protect our natural resources for our children? Or our right to protect our homes? As we started looking into these questions, we found out some noteworthy things about corporations and ourselves.

There is no one who is going to come to our aid. It is up to us to find a solution for ourselves.

We want to share that information with you, and we hope that you will find it as intriguing as we do. Enclosed in this packet you will find a number of short articles that we think piece together a very interesting picture. It is a picture of how our influence, as citizens of the most powerful country in the world, has been taken from us. It is the beginnings of a picture of what we might be able to do about it.

We began by studying the history of corporations in this country. We found that up until the late 1800s the relationship between the people and their corporations used to be quite different than it is today. Over time, corporate leaders found ways to manipulate and change the law in order to protect their own private interests against the interests of the people. We learned the startling history of the regulatory agencies: they were in fact created more than a century ago to weaken the people's ability to protect themselves from giant corporations, which explains why these agencies seldom do an even adequate job of protecting us from the corporations. We found a different way to look at the relationship between a corporation and its workers, one where it makes no sense that workers' rights are always in the shadow of the "rights" of the corporation. We also learned that it wasn't always this way, and we feel compelled to share that with you, and see what you make of it.

We also want to share our proposal towards a solution. We know it looks ambitious, but what else can we do? The mills are almost all closed. The main-stay of our economy has been greatly weakened. Floods are becoming more frequent and more damaging. Our fishing industry has been greatly depleted. Our children's future has been compromised. There is no one who is going to come to our aid. It is up to us to find a solution for ourselves. What choice do we have? Our proposal is simply that, a proposal; and we hope that it starts the conversation. We are not wedded to these ideas, but we do hope we can find ways to be united rather than divided in our response to the situation in our community.

Please share your response with us. We are eagerly looking forward to hearing from you.
Sincerely,

Gil Gregori, Dennis Huber, Paul Cienfuegos, Kaitlin Sopoci-Belknap, Ken Young, and An Anonymous Timber Worker

LETTER TO THE EDITOR: MAXXAM CORPORATION KEEPS BREAKING THE LAW

Sent to the Times-Standard daily newspaper in Humboldt County, California, on October 20, 1998 (Not published. Shall I feign surprise?)

Maxxam Corporation keeps breaking the law in the forest, outraging more and more citizens. The California Dept of Forestry (CDF), which exists primarily to obstruct citizens' rightful authority over the actions of Maxxam and other logging corporations, continues to play its role perfectly. Citizens from all walks of life, including longtime residents of Maple Creek and other impacted watersheds, sense correctly that they have no choice but to enforce and defend the law themselves. The Sheriff's Department, whose entire budget is paid by county citizens, continues to defend corporate property against these very citizens.

The entire regulatory law structure
was created at the turn of the century to shield
corporations from We the People.

How did it come to pass that Maxxam Corporation has more private property protections than actual flesh-and-blood local residents? The answer is quite simple, but remarkable. In 1886, corporations won "personhood" rights which guaranteed them the free speech and private property protections that the founding fathers intended solely for We the People. In fact, the nation's founders were quite clear that corporations were to have no rights beyond what citizens authorized via corporate charters.

Mary Bullwinkel (Maxxam's Public Relations Director) continues to lie in the service of her corporate employer. The Times-Standard (owned by the giant MediaNews Group Corporation) continues to print the lies, and defend corporate property and free speech privileges, while locking out the opinions held by the majority of local people, not to mention basic facts.

If we held the directors and stockholders of these two corporations personally liable (as was the norm in every state until the 1900s) for the ethical and ecological harms caused by these corporations, they'd change their ways mighty fast!

Does the public realize that the entire regulatory law structure (i.e. California Department of Forestry, National Marine Fisheries Service, etc.) was created at the turn of the century to shield corporations from We the People? How long will we allow our corporate creations to run amok and trample our constitutional rights? We must not allow ourselves to be sucked into their hearing rooms governed by their ground rules.

If democracy is to survive in Humboldt County, we all need to learn our revolutionary history so that we can reclaim our sovereign authority over all the corporations which do business here.

For more information, please contact us.

– Paul Cienfuegos, Director, Democracy Unlimited

Chapter Three

Thinking of Climbing Beyond the Outside of the Box? Let's Go!

I'm no longer accepting the things I cannot change ...
I'm changing the things I cannot accept.

—*Angela Davis, academic scholar, author, activist,
and co-founder of Critical Resistance*

Every act of progression in our nation's history has involved tension with law.
Whether it was the abolition of slavery, whether it was the enfranchisement
of women, whether it was the birth of our nation, laws were broken,
and that's because the laws were wrong.

—*Edward Snowden, former CIA employee leaked classified information from the
National Security Agency in 2013. He has been called a hero, whistleblower,
dissident, traitor and patriot.*

Imagining a City
Where Renters and
Property Owners
Enjoy Fully Equal Rights
Under Law

I wrote this as a commentary/podcast for the KBOO Evening News in Portland, Oregon on April 28, 2015. This is an updated version. Although the essay refers to the housing crisis in Portland, Oregon where I live, you could drop your own community's name into this document and it would likely still be entirely accurate!

As listeners surely already know, Portland is fast becoming an unaffordable place for many of us to live. The latest attempt to do something about it is called the Portland Renters Assembly, which the organizers define as "a gathering of people united by the burden of rent." I am excited that renters are getting themselves organized, but as with so many examples of single-issue emergency response activism, I am skeptical that their current work will bear fruit unless they identify and then directly confront the institutional causes of this problem.

As they state in their public documents, "There is a need to stand behind those facing foreclosure, eviction, houselessness, and rents rising well beyond liveability ... The Assemblies discuss the collective strategies to fight back against the exploitation of the human need for housing."

I couldn't agree more, but if we don't wish to waste everybody's time, *how* we stand with each other as disenfranchised people, and *what* collective strategies we choose to explore, are very important issues to figure out.

I'd like to take a crack at reframing what the problem is. Here goes.

Fact #1

A large percentage of Portland residents are tenants with very few legal rights protecting them from eviction or substantial hikes in rent. A small number of people and corporations, some local but many not, own all of the rental housing in Portland.

Questions we need to discuss among ourselves regarding Fact #1

- Why do we, the majority of Portland residents, continue to allow a small number of individuals and corporations to own so much real estate in Portland?

- What are the structures of law that make this disparity of rights virtually inevitable?

Fact #2

Home and apartment rental owners have vastly more constitutionally protected rights than do renters and other non-property owners: namely, they have property rights. In other words, those with property are protected by our current U.S. Constitution, while those who do not own property have no equivalent constitutional rights. In our country and in our current U.S. Constitution, property rights literally trump all other rights.

Questions we need to discuss regarding Fact #2

- Why do we, the majority of Portland residents, continue to allow property rights to trump all other rights?

- Why do we allow corporate owners of property to possess *any* constitutional "rights" when many of us already know that it's ridiculous that corporations are allowed to exercise constitutional "rights"?

- Is it conceivable that we cannot get our rights as tenants fully recognized and enforced until we also tackle these historical realities?

- Can we begin to imagine what a new set of local and state laws might look like where renters and owners would enjoy fully equal and enforceable rights under law?

Fact #3

It is currently illegal in the state of Oregon, and many other states, for local governments to pass rent control and other tenants' rights laws.

Questions we need to discuss regarding Fact #3

- Why do we, the majority of Portland residents, continue to allow the state of Oregon to pre-empt, and thus violate, our inherent right of self-government as enshrined by our state constitution, which states "that all power is inherent in the people, and all free governments are founded on their authority, and instituted for their peace, safety, and happiness; and they have at all times a right to alter, reform, or abolish the government in such manner as they may think proper."

- If all power is, indeed, inherent in the people, why are we not exercising this power?

I would argue that until we are having this larger conversation, we're not ready to mobilize ourselves as tenants.

When governments deny rights to people, those governments themselves become illegitimate, and it is then our responsibility as citizens to alter, reform, or abolish our government in such manner as we may think proper.

Yes, it is a wonderful and very valuable thing for we who are renters to gather together to share our stories about the "burden of rent." It's wonderful for us to learn how to act in solidarity with each other to try to envision how we can unburden ourselves from this economic disparity of the 1% versus the rest of us. But please, let's think bigger and bolder than simply creating yet another activist group of disenfranchised people signing petitions and marching and rallying and picketing and getting angry and making demands and trying to stop no-cause evictions one at a time, endlessly, into the future. We can do better than that! We really can.

Imagine instead, We, the majority of Portland residents, working together in solidarity to envision a series of Portland ballot initiatives that enshrine into law our inherent right of self-government. Specifically, these ballot initiatives could prohibit no-cause evictions; they could strip property owners of any superior rights to those rights held by non-property-owning residents; they could prohibit banks from foreclosing on homeowners who have fallen behind on their mortgages; they could guarantee to all Portland residents the right to have a roof over their heads. These are the sorts of ordinances that we could pass locally by using the strategic framework of the community rights model of locally enforceable law making.

When our state government tells us that we are prohibited from protecting the health and welfare of local renters, the government's position is illegitimate. When governments deny rights to people, those governments themselves become illegitimate, and it is then our responsibility as citizens to alter, reform, or abolish our government in such manner as we may think proper. These are our inherent rights as We the People of Oregon, and it's about time we started to use them again. Yes, it's true, we barely know what these words mean anymore, so we've got a lot of community education that we're going to have to do together. But quite frankly, we have no time to waste. The situation is urgent.

When Will Politicians Start Exercising Their Constitutional Authority to Rein in Large Corporations Like Amazon?

I wrote this essay as a direct response to the progressive cheerleading that appeared across the independent media when Amazon Corporation's directors abandoned their plans to build a second HQ in New York City. It was published in the journal Progressive Populist on July 1, 2019.

Early in 2019, Amazon MegaCorp was all over the news when it announced that it had abandoned its plan to build its second headquarters in New York City. Many progressive elected officials and activist groups from across the country cheered the news, claiming that this would prove to be a turning point in the trend for large corporations to demand huge tax breaks to locate in various places. However, those progressive voices missed a much bigger story because they had forgotten their history. Our nation used to require business corporations to follow very strict requirements and prohibitions if they wanted the privilege of doing business, the privilege of incorporating. Why do we no longer insist on these rules for large corporations like Amazon?

Imagine for a moment if Amazon MegaCorp had to play by the rules that were established for business corporations after the American Revolution and that lasted for almost a century. What might have been different in how its leadership played one community against another for the massive tax breaks and subsidies they demanded? Actually, that's the wrong question entirely, because if Amazon had been around in the 1800s (bear with me here, I know it's a stretch to imagine it) this is what its directors would not have been allowed to do.

The Amazon Corporation would not have been allowed to exercise the First Amendment free speech rights of a corporate person, so it could not have lobbied public officials for any reason whatsoever. Nor could it have publicly opposed, with its corporate voice or its campaign donations, the Seattle City Council's attempt in 2018 to pass a "head tax" on huge companies like Amazon, which would have helped the city to raise more money to tackle its affordable housing crisis. (Amazon Corporation won, the people of Seattle lost.)

The Amazon Corporation would not have been allowed to exercise its tangible property rights, so it could not have purchased any properties without prior consent from Delaware, the state in which it was chartered.

The Amazon Corporation would not have been allowed to exercise its intangible property rights either, so its board of directors and CEO would not have been allowed to make independent decisions regarding:

- how it would compete against other businesses;
- how it would organize its workplaces and treat its employees;
- how it would invest its record-breaking profits;
- which other businesses it would choose to purchase or to destroy;
- how it would redefine the publishing industry; and
- how it would quietly collaborate with various branches of the U.S. government to create one of the most comprehensive surveillance systems the world has ever known, etc, etc.

These are just a few of the many intangible property rights that corporate persons now exercise.

In addition, the Amazon Corporation would not have had legal standing in the courts, so it could not have sued governments, people, or other corporations.

The Amazon Corporation would not have had privacy rights, so the state in which it is incorporated (Delaware) would have had the legal authority to examine the corporation's financial records and other private documents at any time and for any reason.

The Amazon Corporation would not have had constitutional protection under the Contracts Clause of the U.S. Constitution, so the state of Delaware could have chosen to unilaterally amend the corporation's articles of incorporation at any time, to further limit (or expand) what it was allowed to do and to become, or to revoke its very existence through charter revocation.

The Amazon Corporation would not have had constitutional protection under the Contracts Clause of the U.S. Constitution, so the various states could have prohibited it from selling books or building massive fulfillment centers inside their state borders. They could also have placed additional restrictions on it doing business within their states.

I could go on!

The myriad ways in which large business corporations today exercise their so-called constitutional "rights" have become an ongoing crisis of democracy for We the People of these United States. **We citizens never agreed that corporations should be granted corporate constitutional "rights" nor did any of the people we elected grant these to them. The U.S. Supreme Court did that.** Then our federal and state governments updated their statutes to incorporate these new judge-made laws as the new background normal. All without The People's consent, and in a nation that constitutionally requires "consent of the governed" for government to maintain legitimacy. (That language appears in our federal and state constitutions.)

And because We don't know our own history, of corporations historically being defined as our subordinates, required to serve us and to cause no harm, we no longer connect the dots regarding what we can do, what we have the constitutional authority to do, when corporate leaders act like kings.

New York State Senator Michael Gianaris is a progressive politician who represents Long Island City, where the Amazon Corporation was planning to build its new headquarters. He was one of the leading opponents of Amazon's plan. He stated:

> The news for Amazon is that they're not bigger than New York City, at least not yet. They may think that they get to dictate terms to governments, but thankfully, we're not yet at that point … This is actually an important moment, not just for New York, but for our nation. This should be a launching point to discuss the logic of these corporate subsidies that are plaguing the entire country. (See

www.CommunityRights.US/Book for the full article in The Guardian.)

Senator Gianaris is clearly a smart man who cares deeply about his city. Except he doesn't know his history, so his goals are a fraction of what they really ought to be. What he could and should have said was:

This is actually an important moment, not just for New York, but for our nation. This should be a launching point to discuss the logic of corporations being allowed to exercise a myriad of constitutional "rights" that are plaguing the entire country and laying waste to our democratic institutions. We have been allowing huge corporations to dictate terms to our governments for far too long now, and it needs to stop. I will be doing everything in my power to bring our great state into alignment with our too-long-ignored constitutional duties in the immediate future.

How do we change the culture so as to move the needle in this direction as quickly as possible, enabling Senator Gianaris (and many other decent politicians) to make this leap of consciousness?

Many of us around the country are working hard to build the community rights movement. **We understand that, in this moment of ecological and social crisis in the world, it is far too late to tackle one corporate outrage at a time. The fact is that these problems are structural.** We need to learn from our history and bring back these century-old laws that can once again subordinate business corporations, so that they are again required to serve The People, to cause no harm, and for their directors and stockholders to, once again, be held personally and financially liable when the corporation causes significant harm to our communities and the natural world.

There is no time to lose. Let us rethink this moment and begin to imagine much bigger goals for ourselves than merely demanding that our elected leaders no longer prostrate themselves when corporate CEOs come calling. I invite you to learn more about the community rights movement.

The People of Vermont
vs. Monsanto Corporation
and Our Federal Government:
What Should the People Do
When Our Rights
Are Being Violated?

I wrote this essay in a moment of personal outrage and grief about how some of our leading national food safety organizations were squandering a key moment where we could have substantially moved the needle on food safety in this country. I had the distinct goal of getting it published in a number of online news magazines like Common Dreams. None published it, nor had the courtesy to respond, with one wonderful exception: CounterPunch, on August 18, 2016, thus becoming my first-ever published essay in a national online news and opinion journal. Thank you, Editor Jeffrey St. Clair.

Beloved historian, Howard Zinn, once said, "Civil disobedience is not our problem. Our problem is civil obedience ... Our problem is that people are obedient while the jails are full of petty thieves, and all the while the grand thieves are running and robbing the country ..."

We all know he is right. One of the more tragic current examples of how American social movements continue to fall into this trap of civil obedience is how our anti-GMO organizations have responded to Monsanto Corporation's proposed DARK Act, which bans states from requiring the labeling of GMO foods, and which our Congress, Senate, and President

Obama all passed into law over these last few weeks, even though it was opposed by 90% of Americans. Because the DARK Act is now law, Vermont's existing law that requires all foods containing GMOs to be labeled, has been struck down and can no longer be enforced.

For years now, the Organic Consumers Association, Center for Food Safety, Food Democracy Now, and other national and state organizations, have been leading the American people down a path of civil obedience, consistently claiming that, if they can just get more signatures on their online petitions, if they can just get another wave of donations from their millions of supporters, they will continue to win against Monsanto Corporation and its allies. If that were actually true, the DARK Act would not have been passed by an overwhelming majority of both Democrats and Republicans, Obama would have vetoed it, and numerous states would have already successfully banned, not just labeled, GMO foods. So, clearly, something is terribly wrong with the strategy that these anti-GMO groups are asking us to follow. Is there a better alternative? Of course there is!

The voters in dozens of states have successfully overruled the federal government, and pre-empted federal authority, through the ballot box.

For some perspective regarding what We the People should do when our federal government overrules our inherent right to protect our health and welfare, let's go way back to 1996, when California voters passed Proposition 215, legalizing medical marijuana for the first time in our modern history. The law they passed was illegal. It violated federal law. Did you know that? And once it was passed, California's legislature, its governor, its attorney general, its sheriffs, were all required to enforce that new state law, which created what is called a "crisis of jurisdiction." In the years that followed, voters in one state after another passed similar laws, all of them illegal under federal law. But they did it anyway. Fast forward to today, we can see that the voters in dozens of states have successfully overruled the federal government, and pre-empted federal authority, through the ballot box. Imagine if medical marijuana activists had instead spent those twenty years sending online petitions to our federal government begging them to legalize medical marijuana. It would still be illegal! Thank goodness they chose civil disobedience over civil obedience in 1996, by exercising their authority at the ballot box!

Abolitionist Frederick Douglass once said, "Power concedes nothing without a demand. It never did and it never will." Regarding GMOs in our food, where's our demand? Online petitions? Public education campaigns? Ineffective consumer boycotts? C'mon now! **The community rights movement has taught us that if we want to build real political power, we don't beg and plead with our so-called leaders. We exercise our inherent authority to govern ourselves.**

Why are we all so civilly obedient to laws which violate our rights?

So, what's stopping Vermont's government from following a similar path? Imagine if Vermont's governor, state legislature, attorney general and sheriffs were letting the Feds know that they would be ignoring the new federal pre-emption law and moving forward with implementing the state labeling law that they already passed. Imagine if the citizens of Vermont were in the streets, actively supporting their elected officials. **What's the worst thing that could happen? Would the Feds dare to arrest Vermont's legislators and governor?** And, if they did try to arrest them, imagine the democratic uprising that would ensue, across the country. The Feds couldn't possibly win this battle in the court of public opinion. Which begs the question, why isn't this already happening? Why are we all so civilly obedient to laws which violate our rights?

Which brings me back to the Organic Consumers Association, Center for Food Safety, and Food Democracy Now which are all treating the new federal law as an outrage, but as legitimate, rather than as a fundamental violation of our inherent right of self government. Yes, they plan to sue the federal government to challenge the DARK Act, but this will take years and a ton of money, while the public once again gets demobilized, and confused about where ultimate power resides.

Last week, Ronnie Cummins, executive director of Organic Consumers Association, wrote an essay about this issue titled "Corporate Money Defeats GMO Labeling—What Would Gandhi Do?" Given that title, I was hoping that he was finally ready to contemplate a new bolder strategy, one that would have made Gandhi proud. But sadly, I was wrong. Cummins is still stuck in what has come to be known as "the colonized mind." He continues to be convinced that our real power is as consumers. He's dead wrong. **Consumer power is a diversion. In fact, consumer power is a concept that was invented by the public relations industry, as a way to confuse Americans as to where their real power resides, which is as We the People, as citizens, exercising our self-governing authority.**

If you care deeply about states having the right to pass laws to protect the health and welfare of their citizens, I urge you to contact Vermont's governor, state legislators and attorney general, and press them to enforce their existing GMO labeling law, regardless of what our federal government says. Remind them that dozens of states have successfully legalized medical marijuana, even though federal law pre-empts them from doing so. And while you're at it, how about also contacting the Organic Consumers Association, Center for Food Safety, and Food Democracy Now, urging them to shift gears towards a more civilly disobedient set of tactics and strategies, taking their lead from the community rights movement. We the People have an inherent right of self-government. Let's make Gandhi proud.

A Community Bill of Rights
for Portland, Oregon ...
Or Any Community!

A guy can dream, can't he?! This is almost entirely based on actual community rights ordinance clauses from campaigns in other U.S. communities. The ultimate goal would be to place this entire Bill of Rights into our existing Home Rule Charter. Your community or county could do this too! It is a tremendous amount of work to achieve, but the long-term benefits would be extraordinary. Your first step? Find out whether your community or county is already Home Rule, and if it isn't, research how it could become Home Rule. Your second step? A ton of sustained community organizing! Community Rights US can help.

Right to Clean Government: Residents of the City of Portland have the right to clean government, which shall include the right to a municipal legislative process free from corporate control and influence.

Right to Fair Elections: Residents of the City of Portland have the right to fair elections, which shall include the right to an electoral process free from corporate influence and voter suppression.

Right to Constitutional Protections in the Workplace: Employees shall possess United States and Oregon Bill of Rights' constitutional protections in every workplace within the City of Portland, and workers in unionized workplaces shall possess the right to collective bargaining.

Rights for Nature: Ecosystems and natural communities within the City of Portland possess inalienable rights to exist and flourish. The rights of rivers, streams, and aquifers shall include the right to sustainable recharge, flows sufficient to protect native fish habitat, and clean water. The City of Portland and any resident of the City or group of residents have standing to enforce and protect these rights.

Right to a Citizen Managed and Accountable Police Force: Residents of the City of Portland have a right to a police force managed by a civilian police chief overseen by an elected citizen police review commission. Also, and appointed by that review commission, a police ombudsman who possesses independent and investigatory powers.

Right to Be Free from Unjustified Excessive and Deadly Force: All people within the City of Portland have a right to be free from the use of unjustified excessive or deadly force by law enforcement. "Excessive force" shall mean, but not be limited to, law enforcement incidents where there is no active assault of another individual(s), threats to assault another individual(s), or deliberate fleeing from law enforcement. "Deadly force" shall mean, but not be limited to, firearms, tasers, electroshock weapons, and batons.

Right to Community-Run Public Education: Residents of the City of Portland have a right to a public educational system managed by the community, which shall be free from corporate influence. The community-run educational system shall consist of parents, teachers, students, local government, and other residents whose duty it will be to oversee curriculum development, assessment, funding, facilities, and technology. Corporations shall not be allowed to influence, in any way, policies or decisions of the community-run educational system.

Right To Affordable, Safe, and Secure Housing: All residents of the City of Portland have the right to affordable housing, the right to be free from housing discrimination, and the right to be free from unfair housing foreclosure. The City shall ensure the availability of low-income housing stock sufficient to meet the needs of the low-income housing community. People and families may only be denied renting or buying of a dwelling for non-discriminatory reasons and may only be evicted from their residence for non-discriminatory causes. Home foreclosure proceedings shall not commence prior to a determination that no other financing options are available to maintain home ownership, as conducted by a city appointed citizen committee.

Right to Subordinate Corporate Powers to People's Rights: Corporations and other business entities which violate the rights secured by this Home Rule Charter shall not be deemed to be "persons," nor possess any other legal rights, privileges, powers, or protections which would interfere with the enforcement of rights enumerated by this Home Rule Charter.

Enough Already!
Proposal for an
International Campaign
to End U.S. Assaults
on the World's People
and Nature

This is a draft proposal that I wrote many years ago but have never shared publicly until now. It is one of my many fiercely nonviolent campaign ideas that just might have legs if the right skilled people got involved, and if a few hundred thousand dollars could be raised to get it launched. Neither of which has happened thus far.

This is a proposal that I envisioned over the past decade (pre-Trump) to create an internationally coordinated campaign to end the U.S. government's (and corporate leaders') continuing military, political, and economic assaults, once and for all, on the peoples of the world and Earth's other living creatures. If We the People of the U.S. are to be brutally honest with ourselves, we have to acknowledge that there is barely any difference between Democrat and Republican policies on this issue. Poll after poll of the world's peoples has demonstrated that the U.S. government is feared more than any other national government. We are the world's #1 bully. We can change that!

A Brief Campaign Overview

The proposal involves two distinct components, each of which can be organized separately, but which when brought together, creates an international campaign more powerful than the sum of its parts.

Component Project #1

- Creation of a website whose goal is to coax millions of Americans to do two things:

- Register their support for a series of demands on the U.S. government to change its foreign policy in a whole variety of ways from military assaults around the world to its frequent vetoes of UN resolutions, to its corporate-managed global trade agreements.

- Sign a comprehensive pledge form that asks them to commit to one or more levels of activism to oppose current U.S. foreign policy until such time as the U.S. government agrees to abide by the set of demands (as stated above).

Component Project #2

Organizing of a massive worldwide outreach campaign to the world's peoples, their elected leaders (at all levels of government), their civic society organizations, their labor organizations, and the general public, with an urgent plea from the people of the U.S. to the people of the world to come to our assistance in stopping our government from committing any more atrocities in other countries.

We the People of the United States are no longer our government's key constituents. Corporations are!

The opening statement would read something like this ...

We the People of the United States, many millions of us (see our names online), urgently request your active and immediate assistance in helping us to stop our government and the corporate leaders who control it from further assaults on your communities, your sovereign nations, and your natural areas. We are millions of Americans strong, but **our country has been captured by a rolling corporate coup which is threaten-**

ing the survival of our very democracy.

We urgently need your help to bring our nation back into its proper role as good neighbor to the world's peoples and countries. We simply cannot do it without your support! Please help us. The situation is urgent!

Rationale for creating such a campaign

The United States and the world are at a level of political, social, and ecological crisis as has never been seen before in the history of the human species. The situation continues to deteriorate rapidly. Time is running out for our species to save itself on planet Earth. Social movements across the world continue to struggle against (mostly U.S.) corporate and government assaults on people and nature, but their efforts have been generally ineffective.

Most social movements in the U.S. are single-issue focused, and therefore mostly incapable of working together effectively to challenge the primary root cause of this crisis: corporate rule. Additionally, the tactics used by most U.S.-based social movement organizations involve the pleading with (or pressuring of) U.S. governmental and corporate decision makers. From writing endless letters to our elected officials, to asking our corporate directors to be more responsible, these tactics are mostly incapable of challenging the status quo, and in many ways run counter to building effective movements toward democratic uprising. This is because they ignore the reality that real power resides in the people, not in our leaders. **Authentic democracy is built and maintained at the grassroots, as are the institutions which support its flourishing.**

At the same time, vast numbers of people across the world watch the U.S. government in horror as it assaults one nation after another, and they wonder why the American people are not more active in their opposition to their own government's activities and policies. The reality is that millions of Americans are opposed to our government's (and corporations') assaults on people and nature, but we are profoundly isolated from each other because our mainstream media institutions are all owned and managed by giant corporations. Most of our feedback loops are severed, so we don't even know how widespread is our dissent. We are mostly in denial about how far this corporate coup has already impacted our so-called democratic society. Thus, it doesn't occur to most of us to ask for help from the world's peoples to tackle our own problems at home. Yet the reality is, we have no other option left at this time because We the People of the United States are no longer our government's key constituents. Corporations are!

Giant corporations already run our government. They already control both mainstream political parties, they fund our elections, they choose our candidates. They already control the flow of ideas and shape public opinion. They already control our nation's food supply. They already define our energy choices. Corporations are in charge here in the U.S.. They govern us. Yes, their grip gets tighter with each year, but their control is already comprehensive.

We are mostly in denial about how far this corporate coup has already impacted our so-called democratic society.

Imagine how powerful it would be if the leaders of foreign governments, and the leaders of foreign labor unions, and the grassroots members of foreign civic society organizations all understood that millions of Americans were urgently requesting their support to stop our own government's (and corporations') destructive acts around the world. No longer could foreign people's opposition to U.S. government activities be honestly described as "anti-American." **For the first time in history, the peoples and leaders of the world could stand together with the American people (in fact, at the urging of the American people) and against the American government and corporate elite.**

Imagine people and governments and social movement leaders worldwide planning and instituting local and national campaigns to oppose further U.S. government and corporate intrusions in their home places. Imagine federal presidents, prime ministers and parliaments, provincial governments, city councils, mayors, and governors, passing non-cooperation resolutions, in solidarity with (and at the urging of) the people of the U.S. Imagine foreign social movement organizations and labor unions refusing to cooperate with U.S. governmental and corporate activities, refusing to accept U.S. corporate shipments of goods, refusing to allow U.S. military bases to operate on their soil, blocking U.S. corporate development activities, etc. And in so doing, knowing that all of their work against U.S. empire-building was being actively supported and appreciated by the people of the United States, millions of them, and growing larger with every day.

To make this vision a reality, millions of Americans would have to sign their names. A massive list, open to viewing by all. A list of millions of Americans refusing to be silenced. Standing up together with their sisters and brothers around the world saying "Enough!"

Enough U.S. bombing. Enough U.S. killing of innocent people. Enough U.S. vacuuming up of the world's natural resources. Enough U.S. violations of international law. Enough U.S. contempt for UN resolutions. Enough U.S.-led corporate-managed global trade treaties which violate sovereignty of other nation states. Enough U.S. funding of repressive anti-democratic regimes. Enough U.S. financial and political manipulation of other countries' elections. Enough!

Component Project #1 (a comprehensive description)

The website would be designed to hold the names and contact information of millions of Americans. These names would be held in strict confidentiality until the list reached a certain number, like one million. This would provide a level of safety for all of those people who would fear government persecution, or loss of job, or social pressure from peers. Individuals could add their names to the list online, using encryption software, or via mail.

The database would contain many fields of information for each signer. The signer could request that some information not be made public online.

Each person would check off any and all actions they pledged (i.e. promised) to take in support of the list of demands being made on the U.S. government regarding changes in foreign policy. Some actions could begin as soon as they signed on (such as writing letters to the media), while other actions (such as massive sustained nonviolent civil disobedience) would be delayed until there were sufficient numbers of signers prepared to act in solidarity. The list of possible action pledges would be substantial and diverse.

To support the U.S. component of the campaign, it could include:

- speaking personally with at least (circle one) 10/50/100 friends, family, co-workers, and/or neighbors to get the word out about the campaign

- putting a campaign sticker on your car or bicycle

- putting a campaign placard in the window of your home or apartment or workplace

- writing letters to the editor of various newspapers and magazines; local, regional, or national
- copying and distributing at least (circle one) 10/50/100/500/1000 campaign leaflets in your local community
- copying and posting at least (circle one) 10/50/100 campaign flyers on bulletin boards in your local community
- attending local and/or regional rallies and demonstrations, educational teach-ins, speak-outs, etc.
- speaking to local and/or regional and/or national civic organizations and asking them to pass a resolution endorsing the campaign
- speaking to local and/or regional and/or national labor union organizations and asking them to pass a resolution endorsing the campaign
- speaking to local and/or regional government officials and asking them to pass a resolution endorsing the campaign
- attending regular planning meetings to coordinate actions in your local community or region
- attending a nonviolent civil disobedience training workshop in your local community or region
- participating in at least (circle one) 1/2/3/5/10 coordinated and planned acts of nonviolent civil disobedience in your local community or region with others who have signed the pledge
- taking leadership in organizing local and/or regional rallies and demonstrations, educational teach-ins, speak-outs, etc.
- taking leadership in facilitating planning meetings to coordinate actions in your local community or region
- facilitating at least (circle one) 1/2/3/5/10/20 nonviolent civil disobedience workshop trainings in your local community or region

To support the world outreach component of the campaign, it could include:

- writing letters to the editor of various newspapers and magazines outside of the U.S.

- writing and/or phoning foreign civic organizations asking for their support for the campaign

- writing and/or phoning foreign labor union organizations asking for their support for the campaign

- writing and/or phoning foreign government officials (national, provincial, and/or local) asking for their support for the campaign

What else?

What you see above is as far as I got in my conceptualization efforts. If anyone reading this has an interest in moving this idea forward, I would be happy to have that conversation with you!

Chapter Four

Mass Media:
You Love It! You Hate It!
You Want to BE It?
We All Need It!

The smart way to keep people passive and obedient is to strictly limit
the spectrum of acceptable opinion, but allow very lively debate
within that spectrum.

–Noam Chomsky, father of modern linguistics, cognitive scientist,
anarchist philosopher and the world's top public intellectual

A community will evolve only when a people
control their own communication.

–Frantz Omar Fanon, French West Indian psychiatrist and political philosopher

The People of Iowa
vs. Dakota Access Pipeline

Since 2013, I have traveled to rural Iowa, Wisconsin and Minnesota dozens of times to lead community rights workshops and to offer ongoing support to fledgling local groups. While thousands of people were converging on the Standing Rock Sioux Tribe's camp in North Dakota in 2016 trying to stop the construction of the Dakota Access Pipeline, I was actively working with local folks across Iowa, with the same goal in mind.

Anti-pipeline organizing reached a fever pitch that year across Iowa as well. I was very active in those efforts, leading numerous community rights workshops along the proposed pipeline route, which was expected to dramatically impact 18 Iowa counties.

Iowans had just one legal opportunity to stop the pipeline from coming through their state; a public hearing in Boone, Iowa, hosted by the state regulatory body, the Iowa Utilities Board (IUB), on November 12, 2015. Two hundred and eighty people attended the hearing, including ten members of 100 Grannies for a Livable Future, whom I had been training to become community rights activists. Their unusual two-minutes-each testimonies startled the crowd and the IUB as one after another, they questioned whether the Board's decision-making authority was even legitimate, and gave mini lessons on why this fateful decision was rightfully the responsibility of the people of Iowa, who were generally opposed to the pipeline. The following month, the IUB approved the pipeline. (Of course. Shall we feign surprise?)

A few months later, I had the privilege of having my anti-pipeline, pro-community-rights OpEd published in the highly respected daily newspaper, the Des Moines Register, on February 22, 2016. The full text of that OpEd is reprinted below. On the same date, the newspaper published an excellent news story titled "Foes Vow to Fight if Bakken Pipeline Approved" that both mentioned my workshop and included accurate information about our strategy. (This article can be accessed at www.CommunityRights.US/Book.)

Some of the pro-pipeline, pro-Koch brothers legislators in the Iowa House of Representatives went into full freak out when they read my OpEd, and Republican State Representative Ralph Watts quickly wrote an OpEd of his own, attacking me personally, which was published by the same newspaper on March 6, 2016. The full text is printed below.

It is such a rare and wonderful thing to get to personally experience a corporate powerholder defending an anti-democratic stance in such a public way. The 1% usually hides behind the corporate veil. As I wrote to my Iowa anti-pipeline colleagues at the time, "I am delighted to see my editorial get pushback because it means at least some portions of the Iowa state powers-that-be are feeling threatened by what I wrote. And they should be."

As it turns out, Watts was one of the top Iowa Republican leaders of the American Legislative Exchange Council (ALEC), funded by the Koch brothers, which brings Republican lawmakers and corporate leaders together in private sessions, to write legislation which they then try to pass concurrently in as many states as possible.

In response to Rep. Watts' attack on me, I requested the opportunity to respond to him directly in the newspaper with a letter to the editor, but the editor told me they didn't have room to keep printing this back-and-forth debate. The full text of my unpublished letter is reprinted here, dated March 8, 2016. Also, below, you will find two letters to the editor, one published, one unpublished, from other participants in the Iowa community rights movement.

OPINION: IOWANS CAN PROHIBIT PIPELINES IN THEIR COUNTIES

By Paul Cienfuegos. Published Feb 22, 2016, in the Des Moines Register.

Are you concerned that the proposed Bakken pipeline could have significant negative economic and environmental impacts in the 18 Iowa counties where it is planned? Are you concerned that the Iowa Utilities Board will approve this boondoggle, regardless of the fact that overwhelming majorities of Iowans oppose this project?

Did you know that the people of Iowa have the inherent right to overrule whatever decision is made by the Iowa Utilities Board about the pipeline? We the People of these United States are sovereign over our federal, state, and local governments. Our ancestors fought and died for this in the American Revolution. Every state constitution recognizes our sovereignty. Here's the language in the Iowa Constitution's Bill of Rights:

> All political power is inherent in the people. Government
> is instituted for the protection, security, and benefit of the
> people, and they have the right, at all times, to alter or reform
> the same, whenever the public good may require it.

The problem is that "We the People" have forgotten what these words mean, so we continue to allow our government to run roughshod over us. And it gets worse. Beginning in the 1880s, as large corporations were starting to appear on the American landscape, the executives of the railroad companies met privately with the attorney general of the U.S., Richard Olney, and together they designed a new system of law, regulatory law, that would, for the first time, allow large corporations to legally cause significant harm to people and nature. The first regulatory agency Olney created was the Interstate Commerce Commission: "a sort of barrier between the railroad corporations and the people," he said. The public was to be pacified with laws that sounded tough but placed much discretion in the hands of regulators. And who better to lead these new regulatory agencies than the experts in those areas: the leaders of industry! The fox patrolling the hen house.

This new system of regulatory law worked so well to protect corporate players from the public's anger that in the decades that followed, every major industry got its own regulatory agency. Fast forward to today and the Iowa Utilities Board is playing the same game. So, let's not give our power away to the IUB so easily. There is another option.

Across the U.S., communities are standing up and exercising their inherent right to say NO to corporate proposals that are likely to cause harm to their communities. Since 1999, about 200 communities in nine states have passed legally binding and locally enforceable community rights laws that:

- ban specific harmful corporate activities,

- strip that sector of corporations of their corporate personhood and other so-called constitutional "rights," and

- enshrine the inherent right of the community to protect its health and welfare under law.

Communities have banned corporate fracking, mining, water bottling, unsustainable energy development, factory farms, and urban sewage sludge dumping on farmland. About 95 percent of these 200 community ordinances have never been challenged in court.

You don't have to give your power away to the unelected and unaccountable members of the regulatory agency, the Iowa Utilities Board. The people of Iowa are the ultimate decision-making authority in their communities, and have the inherent right to instruct their county boards of supervisors to pass community rights ordinances that ban Dakota Access Corporation from building the Bakken Pipeline through their local counties. It's time to get organized. Join us in Boone for the People's Forum on the Bakken Pipeline on Feb. 28 from 2 to 5 p.m. at Boone High School, to learn how we can unite to protect our communities.

Paul Cienfuegos of Portland, Oregon, is a leader in the Community Rights Movement, and will be leading workshops in Polk, Boone, and Calhoun counties from Feb. 28 through March 8.

IOWA VIEW: DON'T LET IUB'S WORK ON PIPELINE BE UNDONE

By Iowa State Representative Ralph Watts.
Published March 6, 2016, in the Des Moines Register.

The Register published an OpEd on February 23 written by Paul Cienfuegos, an Oregon-based community activist who preaches an anti-government, sovereign citizen message in response to the Iowa Utilities Board permitting discussions on the Dakota Access Pipeline.

Cienfuegos claims this issue can be resolved, to his satisfaction at least, by individual counties and cities taking action of their own. Nothing can be further from the truth or the law in Iowa. Iowa's own attorney general has stated that though counties and local communities can enact local ordinances they cannot be in conflict with state law. Furthermore, as representatives of the people of Iowa, the General Assembly, has granted the authority to regulate pipelines in this state to the IUB. It is well within the legal purview of the board to oversee the open and orderly process that has led to the final permitting discussions on the Dakota Access Pipeline.

For a year and a half, the IUB has presented multiple opportunities for public input and held information-gathering sessions involving all stakeholders in the project. Comments have been submitted, testimonies given, and information has been gathered. Now is not the time for that orderly procedure and lawful action to be abandoned and unjustifiably stirred up by an out-of-state environmental activist, which would be an insult to the hard work the dedicated public servants at the IUB have done to ensure they have all the facts and information to make an informed decision.

We, as Iowans, should not acquiesce to the call to abandon our principles and our laws in favor of beliefs that will only obstruct lawful action. The decision whether the pipeline is approved is reserved solely for the IUB, period. Proposing local or county ordinances to supersede or challenge statewide rulings with the force of state law will not be upheld, as our courts have consistently ruled on such matters.

The Dakota Access Pipeline stands to offer Iowans many benefits, from increased tax revenue from the project to fund infrastructure and public services, to jobs for thousands of laborers and workers through the supply chain. Dakota Access stands to work for Iowa and put Iowans to work. More important, it is an essential element in our country's energy future.

As a state representative and an Iowan, I am proud of our state's constitution. Our representative system of government allows for these decisions to be made by public servants like the IUB, as outlined in the Iowa Code, despite what Mr. Cienfuegos claims. I'm proud of the work these public servants do every day, which they do with the best interests of our state in mind and for the future of every Iowan.

At the end of the day this is the IUB's decision to make, with the facts and information they have, and theirs and theirs alone. Iowans from Sioux Center to Keokuk have made facts and opinions known, often working constructively to find solutions that protect both the interests of private citizens and the proposed project. The majority of Iowans believe we can have both energy independence, and new infrastructure, while maintaining our agricultural tradition and protecting Iowa's farmland. Dakota Access' mitigation plans show this is possible. We should not allow this work to be undone by fringe interests when this lengthy approval process has reached the finish line.

I commend the IUB for their balanced and fair approach to the Dakota Access Pipeline proceedings. In a highly divisive climate this is no easy feat, and the board members have maintained a professionalism and decorum about the process that should be commended. I look forward to their final decision on this important project.

State Rep. Ralph Watts of Adel, a Republican, is an engineer and a small business owner. Contact: ralph.watts@legis.iowa.gov

HERE IS THE RESPONSE I SENT TO THE DES MOINES REGISTER ON MARCH 8, 2016, RESPONDING TO REP. WATTS' OPED, BUT THEY CHOSE NOT TO PUBLISH IT.

There are so many errors of fact in Rep Ralph Watts' Op-Ed about my previous Op-Ed that I quite frankly don't know where to begin.

The community rights movement, now active in dozens of states, is not "anti-government" nor does it preach a "sovereign citizen" message; that's another movement entirely. Yes, it's certainly true that the Iowa Attorney General claims that our locally enforceable and legally binding ordinances, which have now been passed in 200 communities in nine states to stop large corporations from harming local communities, are in fact a direct challenge to state pre-emptive laws. But Mr. Watts misses the larger point entirely. We are passing these local laws because our state governments are continually violating The People's inherent right of self-government, as guaranteed in Iowa's and other state constitutions, so local governments across the country feel they have no other choice than to stand up to these unjust state laws simply to protect and defend their local constituents' health and welfare. Yes, the IUB was required to hold numerous hearings. But amusingly, they are not required to consider the views of Iowa voters when making their decision. "And they call it democracy."

Mr Watts: Have you taken any campaign contributions from Dakota Access Corp or any related pipeline interests? If you have, your Op-Ed in this newspaper constitutes a clear conflict of interest, and you owe it to the voters to withhold any further statements or votes on the Bakken controversy.

I have one final question for Mr Watts: If you're "so proud" of your state's constitution, why do you ignore its most fundamental guarantee:

> All political power is inherent in the people. Government
> is instituted for the protection, security, and benefit of the
> people, and they have the right, at all times, to alter or reform
> the same, whenever the public good may require it.

The Iowa State Legislature is constitutionally required to protect The People, Mr Watts. At least 40% of Iowa voters are adamantly opposed to this pipeline project, which has the potential to cause catastrophic long-term damage to farms and groundwater. Yet you refer to all of these voters as "fringe interests," when in fact the fringe element in this equation is actually the three-member unelected and unaccountable board who are legally authorized to ignore The People's concerns in their final decision.

Finally, allow me to shrink Mr Watts' Op-Ed down to a few sentences, with all disingenuous text removed:

> Those words in the Iowa Constitution guaranteeing all political
> power …to the people are just empty words. Those of us in the 1%
> simply ignore them, and you unintelligent and bewildered voters
> should too. We're taking care of your best interests by leaving it up
> to the political appointees who we've hand-picked to approve pretty
> much every major project that large corporations want to bring to
> our state. So what if the IUB is totally unaccountable to the voters?
> I don't see any problem here. Shut up and go back to your boring
> jobs!
> – Paul Cienfuegos

LETTER TO THE EDITOR: CIVIL DISOBEDIENCE IS KEY ELEMENT TO INCITING CHANGE

by Miriam Kashia, North Liberty, Iowa. Published March 19, 2016 in the Des Moines Register.

State Rep. Ralph Watts ("Don't Let IUB's Work on Pipeline Become Undone," March 7; see page 153) seems to have a problem with the idea of civil disobedience in the name of sustainability being used to right injustices or protect the citizens of Iowa. May I remind him that is what it took to undo slavery, give women the right to vote, move forward on civil rights, and give gay and lesbian people the right to marry whom they love. This is how we create change in a democracy when partisan, gridlocked legislators and our system of law obstructs our legal protections. Because of the community rights movement, 200 communities in nine states have protected their families from encroachment and extraction practices they did not want threatening them.

The Iowa Constitution says "All political power is inherent in the people. Government is instituted for the protection, security and benefit of the people, and they have the right, at all times, to alter or reform the same, whenever the public good may require it."

Paul Cienfuegos has been an educator in this movement for 20 years, and he was invited to Iowa by 100 Grannies for a Livable Future, a growing eastern Iowa organization whose motto is "Educate, advocate and agitate."

LETTER TO THE EDITOR

by Einar Olsen. Fairfield, Iowa. Unpublished. Sent March 10, 2016.

Ralph Watts' Bakken pipeline OpEd embodies what Americans increasingly oppose: excessive government cooperation with corporations, to the disadvantage of most.

Watts' slanted language is disrespectful, and he inaccurately associates Cienfuegos with a "sovereign citizen" message. Homework not done.

Accept something because much work has been done on it? Bakken opponents have done just as much work, invalidating your principle.

Opposing Cienfuegos' right to write: how about freedom of speech?

Coming from out of state? How about Dakota Access? Mr. Cienfuegos is here because not enough Iowans (such as Mr. Watts) understand, and act.

According to Mr. Cienfuegos, Mr. Watts' position is not aligned with the Iowa Constitution.

Oil as an essential element in our country's future? We live in the 21st century, not the 19th.

Most jobs and money from Dakota Access are temporary but potential for expensive pipeline damage is permanent.

If the IUB is an unbiased public servant, why did one of its members allegedly say opposing the pipeline might endanger his political career?

I live in Iowa and honor its constitution, but am not proud of letters like this by Iowa politicians, and encourage all responsible Iowans to study www.NoBakken.com, think it over, and act.

OpEd:
"A National Emergency Requires a Bold Local Response." A Corporate Daily Newspaper Refuses to Publish Yet Another Timely Guest Editorial (Cuz … Ya Know …)

On August 16, 2020, Community Rights US submitted the following OpEd to The Oregonian (Portland, Oregon's daily corporate newspaper) under the title "A National Emergency Requires a Bold Local Response." Unfortunately, but not surprisingly, their Opinion Editor, Helen Jung, rejected our submission with this odd comment: "[W]ith so many op-eds coming in on very timely topics, I don't foresee using it. There's just so much news happening right now and the piece doesn't have quite the urgency or focus." Frankly, it's hard for us to imagine a topic more "timely" or urgent than one that introduces the community rights strategy to tackle our nation's multiple and still growing emergencies, when neither our state or federal government has any clue what to do in this dire moment.

The United States is increasingly a failed state. We are now in the grips of multiple simultaneous emergencies:

- 40% of U.S. renters risking eviction;
- Half of small businesses may never reopen;

- 50 million people are unemployed;

- Epidemic of police violence;

- Upwards of 300,000 Covid deaths by December 2020; and

- Catastrophic climate destabilization.

What are Congress and our President doing to boldly respond? Almost nothing. We cannot afford to continue waiting for government rescue. It's time for Plan B.

Historically, We the People established our federal government and business corporations to serve us, with duties and responsibilities to act in the public interest. Corporations were chartered "to obey all laws, to serve the common good, and to cause no harm." Unfortunately, corporate money and power are now so entrenched in our federal and state governments that our elected leaders no longer serve the public interest.

They used their constitutional powers to protect themselves. But first, they had to become brave and get organized.

Have we forgotten that we are We the People, citizens with tremendous constitutional authority to govern ourselves? In this moment of national crisis, We are the leaders we've been waiting for. Our time to act is now, and our greatest power resides locally.

How do we most effectively organize locally? Since 1999, the community rights movement has assisted 200 communities in twelve states to pass locally enforceable laws. These communities were facing their own emergencies: corporations coming in and (legally!) poisoning their water supply, or (legally!) dumping toxic sludge on farmland, or (legally!) spraying pesticides from the air on farms and forests where people live. They used their constitutional powers to protect themselves. But first, they had to become brave and get organized. We Portlanders can respond just as boldly to our big emergencies.

Portland's City Council passed a Housing State of Emergency Declaration in 2015, enabling additional law-making authority. Our housing emergency is even graver now. We also have a small business closure emergency, and an unemployment emergency, and a police violence emergency. In a crisis of this magnitude, when state and federal governments are either unwilling or unable to protect the citizenry, local governing authority must be utilized to its fullest extent, even if it means challenging so-called "settled law" to do so.

Portland's City Council, or Portland voters, could enact a variety of groundbreaking community rights laws if we begin to take ourselves more seriously by exercising our constitutional right of self-government. Examples include:

- Prohibit residential and business landlords from evicting their existing tenants;

- Prohibit banks from foreclosing on Portland home owners;

- Prohibit utility companies from shutting off essential services to homes and businesses;

- Transfer upwards of 50% of our current police budget towards providing more effective community safety programs;

- Prohibit local police from responding militarily to protests that are protected under the First Amendment;

- Place at least 5% of Portland's annual budget into a newly designed "participatory budgeting" process, and increase the amount by 5% each year.

Unfortunately, our Democrat-led state government continues to move in the opposite direction, taking local power *from* The People. In 2016, Oregon passed SB 1573, drafted by the Oregon Homebuilders Association. This violates Oregon's constitutional guarantee of local "home rule" and self-governance against legislative interference in community affairs. Once again, Oregonians were sold out to the highest bidder by our state legislature and Governor Brown.

We are living through the largest social and economic and environmental emergency since the Civil War.

If We the People are committed to protecting our communities in this moment of extraordinary peril, **the Oregon state government should not be allowed to reduce the decision-making authority of local governments or their residents.**

A community rights local law-making approach is exactly the correct response to such state over-reach.

Just imagine how Portland could become a beacon of light for the rest of the nation. Imagine if other cities followed in our footsteps. Imagine if We the People began to recognize that our most nationally transformative work could be done locally.

We are living through the largest social and economic and environmental emergency since the Civil War. We the People have enormous constitutional authority (and responsibility) to act as the primary decision-makers when our government is failing to do its job.

Are We up for the task? Do We have any other choice?

If you're ready to be part of the change, please contact us: www.CommunityRights.US/Portland.

- Paul Cienfuegos, Founding Director, Community Rights US

- David Delk, National Co-Chair, Alliance for Democracy

- Bryan Lewis, Board President, Community Rights US

Everyone Lives Somewhere So There's No Better Place to Challenge Corporate Media Than in One's Own Community

This essay is a combination of an article that I wrote in 2003 after inventing a new workshop titled "Taking OUR Local Mass Media Back From Large Corporations" which I led in three states, plus portions of a weekly commentary/podcast on the same topic that I presented on June 30, 2015. I would love to hear from anyone who wants to explore what it would take to create this sort of media activism where they live.

I have been concerned for quite some time about the impact of large corporations owning virtually all of our mass media. In my opinion, Americans drastically underestimate the significance of this current reality. **We the People simply cannot do a decent job of participating as informed citizens when most of us have no clue how to locate accurate and comprehensive news and analysis about what is really going on in our communities, our states, our nation, and the world.** Therefore, a functioning democratic culture is close to impossible. This is just one of a number of reasons that I claim that we do not live in a functioning democratic society at all. That in fact, our nation was set up to exclude the vast majority of us from any meaningful participation in our own governance.

Let's just imagine for a moment what might happen if Americans across the political spectrum decided one day that we'd had enough of a corporate media that wasn't doing its job. Imagine if Americans began to understand that rights are for people and other living beings; that the proper relationship between The People and our corporate creations is that we are in charge; and that the corporation has duties and responsibilities to us that it must meet, or else its charter will be revoked and the company dissolved. **Imagine if Americans understood that we must treat media corporations in just the same way as we treat energy corporations and food corporations and insurance corporations: as our subordinates.** Believe it or not, this is actually how it was in the early U.S. history.

If We the People understood our own history, and our responsibility as citizens, how would we act? What would we do, when the editors or publishers or owners of your local corporate daily newspaper or NPR's Morning Edition, or Fox News or MSNBC failed to adequately provide us with comprehensive and accurate news and analysis about the critical issues of the day, as is currently the situation?

At this point, because we treat large corporations as goliaths, rather than as our servants, most of us think that all we can do is beg and plead with corporate decision-makers: "Please sir, may I have some more?." But if we could decolonize our minds sufficiently to see these institutions as our subordinates, as our servants, what changes in our news media would we insist on making?

Last month I traveled to Madison to attend the extraordinary National Conference on Media Reform. Almost 2000 people were in attendance, from Indy Media producers to grassroots organizers, with some really famous folks like Bill Moyers and the president of PBS, Amy Goodman and Juan Gonzales (of Democracy Now), Michael Copps and Jonathan Adelstein (the two dissenting voices on the FCC), Robert McChesney (author of *Rich Media Poor Democracy*), John Sweeney (AFL-CIO president), Al Franken, Studs Terkel, Naomi Klein ...the list goes on and on. It was quite the event! I had the privilege of being one of only ten folks chosen to lead workshops focusing on tactics related to democratizing our media.

Without open and functioning feedback loops that an effective mass media provides, We the People no longer get to know what We the People are thinking.

Just five months earlier, I had begun to facilitate a new workshop that asks participants to contemplate what role they might be willing to play in their own local communities to begin to challenge the legitimacy of the outrageously bad local network news stations and newspapers which now provide almost all local news in this country, and which are almost all now owned by a handful of huge conglomerates like Viacom and Clear Channel Communications. My colleague Betsy Barnum from Minneapolis agreed to co-lead the two conference workshops, "Taking OUR Local Mass Media Back From Large Corporations," which were attended by more than 140 people.

We are in a true crisis situation in this country, where giant corporations now control virtually all aspects of our society, from funding our election campaigns to choosing our news stories and framing the boundaries of the debate, to educating and entertaining our kids, to growing our food, to owning our drinking water distribution systems. (The full list would take pages!) Both the Democrats and the Republicans are now so dependent on corporate money and ideas that we can no longer even honestly say that we have a party of opposition in Washington D.C.

What we need in this enormous country
is a plan of action that is designed to be led
and won at the local level.

When giant corporations own virtually all of our mainstream media, and control our federal government, it is only We the People of this country who are left to figure out how to get our democracy back. This is going to be a very challenging task indeed, for without open and functioning feedback loops that an effective mass media provides, We the People no longer get to know what We the People are thinking. The result is that most of us end up believing that we must be outside of the mainstream of public opinion, since we rarely hear anyone who speaks for us, who voices our own concerns. So we silence ourselves. This is what people do in a totalitarian society, and it is perhaps the biggest catastrophe of all. Can it be that the United States has become such a place? To me and most of the people I know, the answer is a horrifying "Yes!" So, what can the average person do about this? That's what my new workshop is all about.

I am convinced that the most effective place to challenge the corporate media's stranglehold on our society is in the towns and cities where we Americans already live. Yes, we need national groups working to reform federal media policy, but that kind of political action is guaranteed to convince most citizens that the best they can do to participate is to send an annual $25 check to a group most likely based in D.C., and to write an occasional letter to their elected officials. As most people reading this already know, these two activities are stiflingly dull, fundamentally disconnected from the building of real citizen power, and likely to create still more unresponsive top-down national organizations.

Surely, in a democratic society, we can do better than that!

What we need in this enormous country is a plan of action that is designed to be led and won at the local level in hundreds of American cities and towns by millions of ordinary people focusing our collective attentions on our local corporate media offices. These, I might add, are the corporate sites most vulnerable to sustained democratic actions of resistance and disruption anywhere in the U.S. And if these ongoing campaigns in hundreds of communities are well connected to each other in sister-city relationships, is that not far more preferable than one monolithic campaign always trying to rouse the locals with urgent calls for support from above? In other words, if we truly mean it when we say that our goal is to democratize the mainstream media in this country, then shouldn't we be doing our work as democratically as is humanly possible?

As a grassroots community organizer with 26 years' experience, I have come to believe the following ...

1) **All work is ultimately local.** For the ordinary citizen (not the average activist) to comfortably choose to become part of a media reform movement, it would have to be local in its goals, it would have to be led by people living locally, it would have to be created and designed democratically through an open and ongoing program of outreach to the *entire* local community (not just our friends and political allies), and perhaps most importantly, its primary funding would come from those who directly participate in it.

2) **Most Americans, regardless of their party affiliation, age, or location, are extremely concerned about the corporatization of our society and its media.** We are capable of working together, across ideological boundaries, to insist that our local mainstream media in every American community become responsive to the people of that place or be replaced by a

locally controlled institution better suited to meet the needs of the people of that place.

3) The notion that the average American doesn't care about the state of our mainstream media is just plain wrong. What if instead we began to understand (and believe) that, in fact, most Americans don't participate as citizens because they know that their efforts will be fruitless, that their voices will be ignored by the powers that be, that their act of voting just further energizes a corrupt and broken election system. In other words, that they've *accurately* perceived the state of U.S. *democracy*, and chosen to not lend their support to such a charade. I've never met an apathetic American. No, I'm not kidding! Every human being cares, to the extent that they have some control over the outcome of that particular situation. Sadly, for most Americans, the boundaries of such caring have now retreated to the edges of our physical yards and immediate families and friends. It's a tragedy of enormous proportions, but it's more an indication of the state of our society than of the apathy of its citizens.

4) The best way to challenge these giant media conglomerates, and the place where they are most vulnerable to citizen action and disruption of business as usual, is at their thousands of local TV stations and newspapers. These are sprinkled in virtually every city and town across the nation, in other words, where we already live! Activists love to travel great distances to participate in mass actions. The average American does not. Activists have the luxury of being able to leave home for days or weeks at a time. The average American must somehow find the time to squeeze their civic participation into a very tiny number of brief moments of freedom each week.

Therefore, if we are serious about building an enormous movement to challenge the corporatization of our mainstream media institutions, what better way is there than to frame our goals and strategies in a language that resonates with most Americans? It doesn't matter where they stand on the ideological spectrum. Americans can focus their energies on the local corporate media offices which produce the crap that they actually watch and read (and endure) every day: local TV newscasts and newspapers. They can design campaigns which offer truly empowering, exciting, and ongoing opportunities to all participants so that everyone experiences a direct relationship between their collective actions and the results which unfold before their very eyes (and not via mere pictures on a TV screen).

What makes me so optimistic about this strategy for media reform is that this is one of those issues where almost everyone already agrees. We just don't know we do!

Regardless of our worldview, most of us want our news sources to tell us the truth. We want our media to be properly funded so reporters have the resources they need to do an adequate job. We want a firewall between editors and journalists on one side, and advertisers on the other (if we even want advertisers at all). We want the media institutions' decision makers and owners to be held accountable for their actions. We want local control and/or ownership of local media institutions, and we want access to a full spectrum of opinion on the issues of the day.

Now imagine if that yearning could be translated into a demand. And imagine if, in every city and town, that demand was coming not merely from progressive groups, but from thousands of people and organizations across the political spectrum, listing exactly what changes the local corporate media office would be required to achieve, and by what date, if its decision makers wanted to continue to be given the *privilege* of serving that community. Yes, corporations are constitutionally our subordinates with duties and responsibilities to We the People, and state governments have the legal authority to dissolve them if they violate their charters.

Real democratic action, linked to sustained campaigns, can only happen where people live.

Try to imagine how much trust building would have been necessary for people who thought they had nothing in common, until they found out how much they respected and agreed with each other. Imagine how that newly found level of trust would be needed and tested if a particular campaign were to be met with stonewalling by the managers or owners of the local corporate media office. It might possibly require an escalated level of citizen action involving disruption of the institution's day-to-day operations.

Now imagine the exponential potential of this sort of community-based organizing. People in towns and cities in one state would be coordinating their activities with people in towns and cities in other states because they were all challenging the supposed constitutional "rights" of the same massive corporate conglomerates to provide their local news. Imagine the extraordinary power we would have in disrupting business-as-usual in dozens, if not hundreds, of cities in coordinated actions.

Isn't that the sort of mass movement that gets your spine tingling? Isn't it a bit more compelling a campaign to envision than one that merely asks for $25 checks from thousands of Americans who otherwise are given no other opportunities to participate in this extraordinary stuff called participatory democracy?

Real democratic action, linked to sustained campaigns, can only happen where people live; and almost everyone lives somewhere that is currently serviced by a local branch office of a giant media corporation. Let's roll up our sleeves and get to work in our own communities. There is much to do, and the task is truly urgent. **Heck, we may actually discover that we have more in common with our neighbors than we could ever have imagined; and that it's not as impossible as we thought it would be to insist on a mass media that provides, for the first time in a long time, accurate and comprehensive news and analysis from voices as diverse as the American people.**

To learn more about the large corporations that provide the media in your community, you can begin your research by going to www.CommunityRights.US/Book, where key website links are listed.

"Taking OUR Local Mass Media Back From Large Corporations" at: www.CommunityRights.US/Workshops gives more information about Paul's workshop.

Chapter Five

"There is No Time Not to Love"

Song lyric credited to Charlie Murphy

We are caught in an inescapable network of mutuality,
tied in a single garment of destiny.
Whatever affects one directly, affects all indirectly.

*– Martin Luther King Jr, from his **Letter from Birmingham Jail**, April 16, 1963*

It matters not who you love, where you love, why you love,
when you love, or how you love; it matters only that you love.

*– John Lennon, English singer, songwriter, musician, and peace activist
who achieved worldwide fame as a member of the Beatles*

Some Reflections
on 20 Years of Activism,
and An Invitation

I published this essay in the September 1997 issue of Access Journal when I was 39 years old, as I reflected on my first 20 years of intensive social change work, beginning when I was just 18. I am now 63 years young (!) and have spent an additional 24 years of my life still focusing primarily on social change. It is remarkable to me how well this essay still holds up in the craziness of today's world, written at a time when people were just starting to have email addresses!

I became a community activist for social change as an 18-year-old student at The Evergreen State College in Olympia, Washington. At the time, I didn't think of it as a career choice; I just knew I was too upset about the state of the world to not get active. Twenty years later, I'm still plugging along, only now I understand that this work is my life work, and I deserve to get paid a living wage. I only wish more people were ready to join me.

I was an infamous student activist. I organized a successful boycott of the campus food service, led nonviolent direct action workshops against the Trident nuclear submarine, founded a city-wide barter exchange before anyone had personal computers (a huge task!), coordinated an on-campus food co-op, and much more.

Throughout those two decades, I have watched tons of activist friends burn out and never return to social change work. I have witnessed dozens of close friends, who swore they'd never own a car, abandon their own idealism and buy one with much shame. I have watched activist friends charge full speed into a poorly designed or way too ambitious project only to lose faith in themselves. I could go on and on. It has become more and more clear to me that activists take ourselves way too seriously, and demand of ourselves unrealistic expectations concerning our ability to not have contradictory and shadow selves.

Somehow, I managed to survive the long hours without pay because I simply believed so strongly in what I was doing. My resume is an unbelievable (and unhealthy) whirlwind of frenzied activity. Here's an incomplete list of the movements I participated in: organic food, anti-nuclear power and weapons, safe energy, alternative economic institution-building, bioregionalism, feminism, prisoner rights, alternative media, ancient forest protection, ecoforestry, labor solidarity, Native sovereignty, ecological restoration, and finally, in my last few years: reclaiming citizen sovereignty over giant corporations. Whew!

Last year I realized that, after 20 years of this adventure, I might actually know enough about the social change process to help newcomers take the activism plunge. To test my new-found confidence, I offered an evening course last spring at Humboldt State University in Arcata, California titled, How You Can Become An Effective Participant In Nonviolent Social Change. Nine students registered, ages 16 to 71. We all had a wonderful time and we all learned a heck of a lot.

At the end of the course, I wrote a letter to my students sharing with them a few truths that I have learned over the years.

Here's a portion of the letter.

Remember, you are not alone in your concerns about the state of the world! And try not to forget the following seven nuggets.

1) There's no need to reinvent the wheel every time you think of some social change work needing to be done. Chances are someone somewhere is already doing it and could use your support. It is better that you locate them before you spend months developing your ideas and vision! How do you find them? You have a number of options:

- Your community is full of incredible resource people hiding in the woodwork, frequently the elders among you. All long-term activists love to have their brains picked.

- Check out the *Alternative Press Index* in your nearest college or larger library. It's usually found next to the *Readers Guide to Periodical Literature*. The Index monitors hundreds of alternative periodicals from across the world and opens an incredible treasure trove of resources to anyone who looks. If your library doesn't have it, tell them to get it. It is very affordable.

- The internet (for those who are comfortable with it) is another treasure trove of social change links and vision, but don't assume everyone's on the web. To enter the internet world requires joining one of the many service providers. I strongly recommend the Institute For Global Communications (IGC), an international non-profit which links more than 40,000 progressive and green social change organizations in 133 countries.

- And of course, there's always picking up the phone and calling me! I'm happy to help.

2) Consumers are workers, are taxpayers, are citizens, are all of us. These aren't separate categories of humanity! When workers strike, and their employer or the government claims that the public is suffering and why aren't those lazy workers more sensitive to the public's needs, remember that those workers *are* the public and they're already suffering or they wouldn't be on strike. (This month it's UPS employees.) Their issues, at first glance, may not appear to be personally relevant to you or to your issue, but look again. We are all in this together. If we each make a conscious effort to support each other's activist concerns, and attend each other's forums and rallies and demonstrations, we will quickly discover that we're all just citizens with surprisingly broad bases of agreement. It's okay if you show up not fully understanding the issues. You'll learn something, and probably even widen your circle of friends.

Remember, you're not apathetic so don't assume anyone else is either.

3) We may all be in this together, but those of us who are black or female or poor or gay or disabled or old or non-English speakers don't necessarily trust those of us who are white or male or financially comfortable or straight or able-bodied or English speakers. So, in order to build authentic alliances across these barriers, we may have to (we may actually *want* to) get to know these folks personally, to learn about their lives, loves, struggles. So, try not to make too many assumptions about our "unity" until you've made a real effort to walk in their shoes for awhile.

And you (i.e. we!) white guys: I strongly encourage you to remember always that you carry loads and loads of invisible race and gender privilege which if not acknowledged and periodically struggled with will almost inevitably sabotage your attempts to work with those not white or male. (Believe me, none of us are exempt, even us sensitive new age guys!)

The institutions that run this society are profoundly good at keeping most of us feeling hopeless, powerless, isolated, despairing, and frightened.

Another angle from which to examine this: **Almost everyone you will ever meet, at work, at the movies or shopping, is "working class."** Be they poor or comfortable, they make up the approximately 85% of Americans who work for a living. They are us! You'll never even catch a glimpse of the approximately 2% who rule us! When is the last time you bumped into the head of your region's largest logging company waiting in line at the bank, or the president of your local college in the aisle at the food co-op? You probably never will; these people live very different lives!

4) Don't believe what the media corporations tell you (duh). Their primary goal in life by definition is to grow and grow and grow and sell you (audience share) to other corporations who wish to advertise their wares to you. That's really all they exist for. It's not all that relevant that what they market is news, they could just as easily be marketing shoes. So bite the bullet and make a $75 or $100 a year financial commitment to keep at least two or three independent green/progressive newspapers or magazines or specialty journals alive. These tiny powerful voices need our support more than ever. One effective way to figure out which periodicals to support is to frequently look up the subjects you're most concerned about in the *Alternative Press Index* and see which sources regularly cover those topics; or go to your local independent bookstore and see what's on the rack. If you're looking for some suggestions, try Z Magazine, Earth Island Journal, and Rachel's Environment and Health Weekly (for starters). You may find it hard to believe, but this nation has the largest selection of progressive and green general interest and specialty magazines of any country in the world, and most people don't even know they exist!

5) Remember, *you're* not apathetic so don't assume anyone else is either. The institutions that run this society are profoundly good at keeping most of

us feeling hopeless, powerless, isolated, despairing, and frightened (which is very different than apathetic), and not the kind of qualities that make good grassroots leaders. So our work, if we're up to it, is to acknowledge that we're all wishing to make a difference in the world, but we have lots of crud getting in the way. Offer others the tools and support they need to once again take the risk of caring enough about our society to get involved. It's a big job, but you folks reading this article are as qualified to do this as anyone else!

6) Social change takes time. Don't expect to see grand changes in the next five years. The really big changes, the ones that happen in peoples' thinking, can often take a few generations. Patience is a profound virtue in an activist. Practice patience daily. And learn how to breathe properly. It really helps when it feels like everything is going to hell.

7) Lastly, think about joining one of the many social change groups in your community. You'll be surprised how many there are tucked in the cracks of your town! And most of them are probably hungry to meet new committed and energetic people like you! I'm a relative newcomer to Arcata and have been shocked to discover that there are 61 local groups here doing wonderful work.

All the best in your work for a healthier, more just world!

How to Set Up
an Economically Dynamic
Sliding Scale Payment System
for Your Events

Every time you pay to attend a conference or a gathering or a training or even a live performance, those who are lower income end up subsidizing those who are higher income. It's counter-intuitive but it's true! And it is patently unfair. I have an elegant solution that is guaranteed to shake things up and make people feel uncomfortable, for all the right reasons!

Way back in the 1980s, I got tired of having to miss so many significant trainings and conferences and workshops and other events, simply because I could not afford to pay what they were charging. I knew that the organizers had no idea that their events were so much less successful than they could have been, with so many lower income people excluded from attending. Events where a very diverse set of attendees would have created a deeper and richer experience for everyone, were instead highly homogeneous, at least by income and class.

In the U.S., we mostly take it for granted that events such as these will be attended almost exclusively by those who have relatively large disposable incomes. Which tends to exclude a majority of people! Class is one of the very last "isms" that our society seems unwilling to directly confront. Somehow, if you're lower income, it must be your fault or your choice; and if you work hard enough, you too can be rich. Which frankly is absurd.

So when an event organizer charges attendees $500 for a weekend intensive training or conference, those of us with low incomes likely cannot attend. And if we feel that we absolutely must attend, in order to further our training or life passion, we have to really struggle to come up with that much money, whereas middle and higher income people pay the cost without even a second thought. This is patently unfair. And the event suffers too, as the life experiences of a diverse population do not end up being represented by those in attendance.

What almost no one seems to realize is that someone who can only afford to pay $100 for the event, but ends up struggling to pay $500, is in effect subsidizing the person who could easily afford to pay $1000 or more for the event, but doesn't have to. So in the early 1980s, I started to work on designing a Sliding Scale payment system that would take these realities into account. I wanted higher income people to have to pay $1000 or more, so that they too would have to think carefully about whether this event was important enough for them to spend that kind of money. I wanted lower income people to start having to pay $100 (or sometimes even less) because that was truly all that they could afford. It seemed so sensible to me. But every time I approached an event organizer with my designed system, they weren't interested. For them, the status quo was working fine. Besides, no one should have to pay $1000 for their event. They simply could not see the unfairness built right into the existing status quo.

Finally, after a few years, I found a group that was willing to experiment with my Sliding Scale design. Beginning in the early 1980s, Interhelp was a growing newly international movement of people surrounding Joanna Macy, Chellis Glendinning, Fran Peavey, and others who were examining the devastating psychological and emotional and spiritual impact of living in a world threatened with imminent nuclear war. I had become a very active member, having recently co-founded Interhelp-UK, the first-ever chapter of Interhelp outside of North America. I flew home from Scotland to attend one of their multi-day gatherings.

The organizers of this gathering had agreed in advance to an experiment, and they asked all of the hundreds of attendees to fill out a form I had created. The form would determine their proposed fee for attending. I still remember it all so well. Because we were a group that was committed to building deep community and being as transparent and real with each other as possible, we even scheduled a mid-gathering evening where everyone would sit together in a comfortable large room, and have an opportunity to talk about how it had felt to be asked to pay way less or way more than they had ever paid for such an event. I was asked to facilitate.

Classism is still one of those topics that is taboo to discuss.

My strongest memory of that evening was of an older very wealthy woman who shared with the rest of us how shocked she was when the form asked her to pay (I believe it was) about $900 to attend. She was used to paying just a few hundred dollars. But over those first few days of the gathering, she noticed a new level of richness of experience in each of the sessions, and began to understand that what she was witnessing was a gathering of her peers that more accurately represented the full community, both wealthy and poor, for the first time ever in this community. Through her tears, she said very clearly that if she had to pay a lot more money to attend these gatherings in order that the events themselves would provide a deeper and richer experience for everyone through massively expanding the diversity of attendees, that she was all in. I remember feeling so proud of that group of people that night.

There were also many folks present who were asked to pay close to nothing to attend, and they too were shocked at what amount the form had recommended that they pay. Some of them felt like they were cheating the system, and yet they also acknowledged that they really couldn't have paid much more to attend, without significant hardship.

The form that I created factored in variables such as:

- how far the person had to travel to attend, given that longer distance travelers were already having to pay significant travel expenses,

- how many dependents the person had that they were supporting with their income, and

- whether there were other income earners in the household.

As intended, the Sliding Scale system that I designed brought in enough money to cover all of the necessary expenses of the event. It was a smashing success.

With this experience, I fine-tuned the form I had created, and started searching for other groups who would be open to giving this a try. But overwhelmingly, what I found was event organizers who were too afraid to implement a sliding scale system.

Since that Interhelp gathering in the early 1980s, I believe I have only found two other multi-day events that were open to utilizing my Sliding

Scale system. As I stated earlier, classism is still one of those topics that is taboo to discuss; much more than racism, sexism, ageism, or homophobia. We in the U.S. want so desperately to believe that we live in an economically fair society. Unfortunately, that is one of our huge remaining societal myths.

Ever since I began to lead community rights weekend training intensives around the country, I have always made a point of asking the local host organizers whether they are open to running the training on a sliding scale basis. More often than not they are willing, given that I am the workshop leader!

I have massively simplified the form that I now use, in order to create a lot less anxiety in the attendees. The form makes it crystal clear, as it always did in the past, that the dollar amount that they are being asked to pay is merely a suggestion. That no one knows better than the attendee what they can reasonably afford to pay to attend. Regardless, this system that I have created always tends to generate a lot more economic diversity in who shows up for my workshops. That's a really important thing, when we're diving deep into discussing how we're going to strengthen participatory democracy and take our society back from rule by large corporations!

If we are truly honest with ourselves about how wide is the gap between higher income people and lower income people, we need to analyze what that ratio is between those income groups. In any large group of people, the annual incomes tend to range from about $15,000 to $150,000. That is a ratio of about 1 to 10, which is generally written as 1:10. Therefore, I always urge anyone who is planning to utilize my Sliding Scale design to implement a sliding scale ratio of at least 1:5, so as to acknowledge the economic reality that is our very unequal society. (You could choose to set up a 1:10 sliding scale ratio for your event, but I guarantee it will freak out a lot of folks! So I tend to go with 1:5.)

Please note that this system does away with the need for scholarships or work trades for low income people, both of which I consider economically discriminatory, and which require the lower income person to request special treatment and to have to come "out" as poor. Many poorer people feel shame about their economic status, so it makes no sense to make them have to request special assistance. I even once set up a work trade system for a quite expensive week-long training where both high and low income people felt it was to their advantage to work off part of their fees, so rich and poor found themselves in the kitchen together, cooking and washing dishes at the training. That was a victory for economic justice.

Here is the text of what I send to the host organizers of the trainings I lead, for them to use in their outreach to potential attendees. As you will note, you can raise or lower the highest and lowest fees in this scale, depending on what amount of money you are trying to raise to cover all of your event expenses.

SLIDING SCALE FEES

I would like you to consider paying a bit more than you are used to paying if you are in an upper income bracket, and a bit less than you are used to paying if you are in a lower income bracket. In this society, we tend to forget that lower income people have much less disposable income for extras of any kind than do higher income people. So what ends up happening is that lower income people actually end up subsidizing the participation of higher income people at events where everyone pays the same price to attend.

If you have lots of dependents, please consider paying a bit less than the amounts listed below. If you have few or no dependents, or you are a multi-income household, please consider paying a bit more than amounts listed below.

If you are at all uncomfortable with my suggested fee scale, please pay whatever amount you feel is right for you to pay. YOU are the best judge of what you can afford to pay. We cannot hold your spot in the workshop until you send payment. Thank you!

This sample fee structure would be used for an event that would have normally charged a set price of around $75. For an event that would have charged a flat fee of about $150, you would double all of these dollar amounts.

Please feel free to contact me if you are considering organizing a major event and want my assistance thinking about a sliding scale fee structure: Paul@CommunityRights.US.

- If you make less than $15,000 per year, please consider paying $40 or more:

- If you make $15,000 to $25,000 per year, please consider paying $70 or more.

- If you make $25,000 to $40,000 per year, please consider paying $100 or more.

- If you make $40,000 to $70,000 per year, please consider paying $130 or more.

- If you make $70,000 to $100,000 per year, please consider paying $170 or more.

- If you make $100,000 or more per year, please consider paying $200 or more.

Imagine if ...
The Great Turning Meets Community Rights (Thank You, Joanna Macy!)

Since 1999, the Community Rights movement has been spreading across the United States, one city, town and county at a time. 200 communities have passed new-paradigm laws that strip corporations of all of their so-called constitutional "rights," ban a variety of corporate activities which are fully legal but considered harmful by the local residents, and enshrine the inherent right of a community to govern itself. These laws are a direct challenge to a variety of structures of law that have made it literally illegal for local communities to protect their own health, safety and welfare. Thus, each of these local ordinances is in itself an act of municipal civil disobedience. The Great Turning provides us with a framework for the essential steps We the People must take to begin to transform our world:

We Change the Ground Rules

- No more playing on a corporate playing field with corporate rules (such as regulatory law & agencies).

- No more battling one corporate harm at a time, endlessly, into the future.

- No longer allowing corporations to operate if they cause significant harm to people and nature.

The primary purpose of environmental regulations is to regulate environmentalists. The primary purpose of labor regulations is to regulate working people.

We Learn Our History

- For our first century after the American Revolution it was still legal for states and local communities to pass laws that protected themselves from harmful corporate activities, because corporations were considered subordinate institutions. What can we learn from the American revolutionaries, the Abolitionists, the Suffragists, the Populists?

We Define Ourselves

- We are not merely consumers and workers. We are "We the People." We are the sovereign people. We are guardians of life for present and future generations. It's not just what do we think we can get. It's what do we want!

- Corporations are not "good corporate citizens." They are merely private property, legal fictions, business structures, and we must again define how they are allowed to operate, as we once did for a century after the American Revolution, in order to protect the health, safety and welfare of our communities and of nature. To do this, we must also reclaim our language from corporate culture.

We Govern Ourselves

- Corporations have become a cancer on the body politic. They have to be removed from all political participation. No corporate money in politics. No lobbying. No corporate "educating" of citizens. No funding of non-profit organizations, or of scientific research. We the People have an inherent right of self-government.

We Meet Our Collective Needs Democratically

- We don't need Safeway Corp to feed us. We don't need Fox Corp and MSNBC Corp and PBS Corp to tell us the news. We don't need Disney Corp to entertain us. We can provide all of our necessities through democratized and accountable business structures, and through a citizen-controlled media.

- We the People must reclaim our self-governing authority, allowing the creation of business institutions only when their directors agree to protect our communities, working people, and nature.

We Define What We Want, and Prohibit (Rather Than Regulate) What We Don't

- Most environmental and labor regulations are written by the industries being "regulated." Corporations haven't "captured" these agencies. They didn't have to. They helped *design* them! Corporate leaders are then chosen (by our presidents and governors) to run the very agencies that are being regulated. You can't make this stuff up!

- The primary purpose of environmental regulations is to regulate environmentalists. The primary purpose of labor regulations is to regulate working people.

- Let's stop playing the regulatory law game, and instead start *defining* what we want and *prohibiting* what we don't. We the People once exercised this very authority after the American Revolution. We can do it again!

Thoughts about Breathing and Not Breathing During This Time of Escalating Emergencies Facing the Entire Planet, and Where Our Energies Can Best Be Focused

I presented the following keynote speech at the Oregon Unitarian Universalist Voices for Justice Annual Meeting in Portland, Oregon on September 19, 2020 via Zoom. The conference took place just weeks before the 2020 general election, and you could sense the general panic in the air, for so many different reasons. If you prefer, you can listen to the speech at www.CommunityRights.US/Book.

I have been thinking a lot about breath lately, about breathing and not breathing. My father died one and a half years ago, in Bellingham, Washington, at the age of 95. Even though he was unconscious his last few days, he waited to take his final breath until I was in the room, holding his hand and talking to him, after I had raced there on an Amtrak train to be with him.

In March, 2020, those of us who live in the United States started to take notice of a strange and scary virus that was starting to sweep across the world. Within weeks, massive numbers of us were dying. One of the first things that became obvious was that the virus attacked a person's ability to take a breath.

Not too many more weeks after that, George Floyd was murdered by four policemen in Minneapolis. Some people in the Black community called it a lynching. **He kept pleading with the cops, saying he couldn't breathe.** More than 6,000 Black people have been lynched by White people between 1865 and the present day. Lynching is the ultimate terror weapon, as it strangles the victims until they die, unable to breathe.

The Movement for Black Lives had already been building up steam for five years at that point, and the local Twin Cities group had been laying the groundwork for much larger scale organizing during those years. So, when the police murdered George Floyd, the Movement was able to immediately mobilize a massive public response, which rapidly spread across the country, like a virus.

I had already attended many Black Lives Matter rallies here in Portland before this latest social eruption. The sign that I always carried, slung around my neck, included the words, "I can't breathe!" This exclamation originated from the police murder of Eric Garner in New York City in 2014. Eric was thrown to the ground and placed in a chokehold. In Eric's final moments of life, he pleaded with the cops, saying, "I can't breathe" eleven times.

Almost exactly one month ago, millions of California residents found themselves living in a dystopian hellscape filled with the smoke of hundreds of wildfires. The sky turned orange. The sun disappeared. Millions of people could no longer safely breathe outside and they became environmental refugees in their own homes. At least the lucky ones did. The tens of thousands of homeless Californians weren't so fortunate.

Just two weeks ago, residents of Oregon and Washington experienced a similar fate. Again, more than a million of us could not breathe, as wildfires raced down mountain valleys, pushed by unimaginably strong hot winds. Yesterday, those of us living in the number one worst air quality in the world here in Portland finally got a reprieve from the suffocating smoke. It rained. Thank goodness it rained! We could breathe again.

I feel like I have been holding my breath for 11 days straight. Now for the first time in my life, my whole body understands what it must be like for those poor souls who live and work in industrial cities in China and India, who have to breathe foul air for much of their lives. To a large extent, they struggle to breathe because their cities are manufacturing that toxic crap that

We *first worlder*s buy to try to convince ourselves that we are happy. This too must stop!

Then, just yesterday, after only half a day of joyous recovery of breath, with windows flung wide open, my breath suddenly narrowed yet again when I heard that Ruth Bader Ginsburg had just died. I couldn't even feel pure sorrow about her death, or feel joy about her extraordinary life, because my mind immediately raced forward to what I knew was coming next.

With not a second to spare, Senator Mitch McConnell was already planning a rapid launch of another Supreme Court nomination process to replace this gem of a human being, Ruth Bader Ginsburg, who took her last breath yesterday. Shame on him! Just thinking about this *pisses* me off. And once again, I can't breathe!

So, many of us were already feeling traumatized by these past four years of Donald Trump as our … as our … sorry I can't say it. I can only refer to him as Resident Trump. He doesn't deserve the P word in front of his name. He hasn't earned it.

The presidential election is just 45 days from today! I know absolutely nobody across the country who isn't feeling a great deal of panic about what is going to unfold on Election Day, and in the days and weeks after Election Day. I personally know a lot of folks across the country, because for many years now I have been crisscrossing the country leading workshops and giving talks as a national leader of the community rights movement. That is, until Covid struck and life changed virtually overnight.

In the days after November 3rd, Trump might refuse to leave office. He might declare martial law. There might be battles in the streets between armed factions of citizens. And that's only if he loses. If he wins, the steady drift towards corporate fascism will continue. It's frightening to even try to imagine what the U.S. will be like after another four or more years of Trump. Just thinking about this, which I do every single day, makes me feel, once again, like I'm holding my breath. I'll bet many of you are having a similar experience.

Black people and other people of color are used to feeling short of breath. They are used to experiencing violence, living with trauma pulsing through their veins their entire lives. But for White folks? This level of trauma is a new experience. Every day seems to bring another traumatizing news story.

Just in the past few days, hundreds of thousands of migratory birds have literally fallen out of the sky in Southwest states. "They're literally just feathers and bones. Almost as if they have been flying until they just couldn't fly anymore," said a graduate student in New Mexico who has been collecting carcasses.

I don't know about you, but every time I hear about a massive die-off of different species, I feel like I am suffocating, as if I cannot access the air I need to simply breathe. And scary ecological news just keeps on coming.

Just this past week, the United Nations reported that the world has failed to meet a single target in the last decade to stem the destruction of wildlife and life-sustaining ecosystems. Wildlife populations are in free fall around the world, driven by human overconsumption, population growth, and intensive agriculture. All of these creatures stopped breathing! Since 1970, global populations of mammals, birds, fish, amphibians, and reptiles have plunged by 68%. Just in the past fifty years.

Of course local communities have the right to protect themselves!

Massive police violence, hundreds of years of white supremacist culture disguised as background normal, huge corporations out of control across the planet, widespread collapse of entire ecosystems, catastrophic climate destabilization, the economic collapse of working families everywhere, a continuing Covid-19 global crisis.

Are you remembering to breathe?! … or are you holding your breath?! This is painful stuff!

And yet, in my increasingly long life on this planet, 62 years and counting, I have never before seen this scale of social movement organizing! Never! The public is mobilizing itself like it never has before. The rabble are rousing! It's very exciting to watch and to participate in.

But time is short. We truly have no time to lose. We have to think carefully, reflectively, deeply, about where to put our energies and money and time for maximum impact.

For me, it's very clear. I absolutely believe that the community rights movement offers us the most effective strategy for solving these enormous problems, which is why I have been active in it for more than twenty years.

For those of you who are not already familiar with the community rights movement, we help communities across the country to pass legally and historically ground-breaking laws that put democratic power and authority back in the hands of local majorities of residents and their local elected officials. We help communities to push back against state and federal governments when they claim that local communities have no right to protect their own health, safety, and welfare. We don't buy that for one second! That's a ridiculous notion, and our organizing strategy is based on refusing to accept that absurd concept. Of course local communities have the right to protect themselves! In fact, that right was among the most important aspects of why there even was an American Revolution.

The right of local community self government was baked right into the revolutionary fervor but the ruling elite of this country has since buried that widespread understanding, that powerful demand from the citizenry. We are here to give that demand water and air again, so that it can put down strong roots and sprout once more, reaching towards the sky. So that We the People can freely breathe again.

In the community rights movement, we understand that we find ourselves in a most urgent situation. It is so urgent that when the federal government refuses to protect and defend the health and welfare of our nation's people, and the natural world that sustains all of us, We the People have to act. When our state governments do not have the resources to offer similar protection, We as the sovereign people must exercise our constitutionally guaranteed authority in the places that we live, be they cities, towns or rural areas. We the People must do this because no other scale of government is doing the job that it is constitutionally required to do. Our federal and state governments are utterly failing us, week after month after year. That is why the community rights movement is sprouting up all over the country.

The community rights movement has already assisted more than 200 communities in 12 states, both conservative and progressive, helping them to pass local laws that stop corporations and governments from forcing harmful activities on those communities. **Our movement helps communities make the bold claim that people, not giant corporations, should be the sole decision-makers as to how a community designs and unfolds its own future.**

Those of us who live in this country have been obedient to unjust laws for far too long. We have allowed giant corporations and our government to ignore our urgent pleas for protection. We simply cannot wait any longer for our so-called *leaders* to lead us. Because in fact, We are the leaders we've been waiting for.

What does this mean for Portland? How would the community rights movement assist the people of this wonderful city? Well … the first step is to begin to envision what it is that we actually want and urgently need for our city.

Today, Portland is experiencing numerous crises and emergencies. We are on the verge of a mass eviction of renters and homeowners. We're on the verge of about half of our beloved small businesses closing their doors permanently. Massive numbers of residents are out of work, with little if any government support forthcoming. Our police force is literally out of control, refusing to abide by the guidelines set forth by our newly-elected district attorney. There is a fast-growing ecological crisis unfolding all around us, in our local forests, our farmland, our wetlands, our rivers.

Believe it or not, We can start, meaningfully and boldly, to address all of these issues through the community rights local law-making process and legal strategy. It's time for our city council to start passing community rights laws that can begin to turn this giant ship around. Voters can also pass these laws directly through local ballot initiatives. Here are some examples of what could be passed into law here in Portland, or *any* community or county for that matter:

- We could place at least 5% of our city's annual budget into a new-ly-designed "participatory budgeting" process that gives all local residents an opportunity to envision how we want our hard-earned money spent. Numerous cities across the US and beyond are already doing this with great success and massive public involvement.

- We could prohibit residential and business landlords from evicting their existing tenants for as long as the Covid crisis continues.

- We could prohibit utility companies from shutting off essential services to homes and businesses, which will be even more essential as winter approaches.

- We could prohibit local police from responding militarily to protests that are protected under the First Amendment.

- We could pass a whole new variety of taxes on the ultra-wealthy, on corporate profits, on stock transactions, on gasoline sales, etc.

and pour that vast amount of wealth into the effective social service programs that prior budget cuts eliminated.

- We could fund state-of-the-art public transit improvements that would actually succeed in getting most of us out of our cars entirely.

- We could begin to provide comprehensive services to help our homeless community to get back on its feet.

- We could begin again to build public housing that low-income residents are proud to live in.

- We could require that all of our grocery stores begin to sell a larger and larger percentage of their products in truly reusable or genuinely biodegradable packaging, in order to end our utterly outrageous dependence on single-use plastic packaging.

And that's just for starters! I want to hear from many of you during our Q&A time together. What are some of your bold ideas for local law making? Ideas that could begin to profoundly change how we live here in this very special but very endangered city.

Our federal and state governments are not coming to rescue us.

Can we deepen our neighborhood connections and reclaim more of our urban landscape as the commons (i.e. commonly shared lands as opposed to privately owned)?

Can we transform our police force and our prisons away from punishment and violence-based solutions?

Can we re-wild our urban landscape to encourage local wildlife to inhabit our city by day-lighting our buried creeks, eliminating toxic discharge entirely, and by de-paving many of our streets?

We the People of Portland can do all of this and more if, and it's a really big if … if we are finally ready to recognize that we truly are out of time, both socially and ecologically. Our federal and state governments are not coming to rescue us. They simply are not! It's up to us, wherever we live, to take the bull by the horns and become the leaders we know we need to be. It's time to stop begging and pleading. It's time to exercise our constitutionally guaranteed self-governing authority. It truly is up to us.

And once we begin down that understandably scary new path, as we re-learn the skills necessary to practice genuine local democracy together, I can offer you one guarantee. We will start to breathe again, more deeply, more calmly, more fully than before. We will *conspire* together, which literally means, "to breathe with"! Because we will have reclaimed our very lives, in community together, where all of us belong.

Thank you!

Learning to
See Each Other
as We the People:
A Guided Visualization

This is a Guided Visualization that I wrote decades ago, loosely based on Joanna Macy's guided visualization, "Learning to See Each Other." I have led it at church services and at workshops all across the U.S.

We the People are awakening to our true collective power, more every year. Not merely as consumers who vote with our dollars. Not simply as single-issue activists, fighting one corporate harm at a time. But as the majority in a society based on majority rule. As the sovereign people, with the constitutional authority to govern ourselves.

Imagine what it might look like, what it might feel like, if We the People started exercising our right to define what we want our communities to look like in five years, in ten years, in 50 years, perhaps even seven generations into the future. I'd like to close this book of mine with something a bit different! May I lead you in a guided visualization, to give you an opportunity to create a picture in your mind and in your heart, to imagine this happening where you live? I call this visualization exercise, "Learning to See Each Other as We the People."

Of course, I can't be with you in this moment, so instead I've recorded myself guiding this visualization. Please go online to www.CommunityRights.US/Visualization, and you can listen to me guiding you through this peaceful process of inner discovery.

Once you've done this with me, I'd love to hear how it was for you. You are welcome to email me at Paul@CommunityRights.US. Thank you!

A Guided Visualization

Please feel free to share this guided visualization with others in your life. You can have them play my recorded voice, or you can read it to them. If you read it, please take a short pause every time you see the row of dots. The entire guide is copied below:

Please close your eyes, and take a few long deep slow breaths …

I'd like to ask you to keep your eyes closed for a few minutes, and imagine that you are standing outside your front door looking around the place where you live. Perhaps there's a row of houses or apartments all around you. Perhaps you live in the country, and can't see another house from your front doorstep. Just rest there for a moment outside your front door …

Now imagine that you are looking into the eyes of one of your neighbors who you barely know but have been curious about for some time … Picture yourself starting a conversation with them, about something that really matters to you. Something going on in your community. It could be something you're really pleased about. Or something that you're really concerned about. Something local to where you live … Imagine stretching beyond where you would normally take a conversation with someone you don't know very well …

Now imagine finding enough courage inside of yourself to share with that person a hope or dream you have about your community becoming much more democratic … where every resident has a voice that matters … where every resident has a natural and easy understanding that their participation in the governing of their home place matters …

[LONG PAUSE]

Now picture your neighbor finding enough courage to share a hope or dream with you that they have about the place where you both live … They too yearn to live in a community where people are more active, more involved, more connected, more trusting … How does it feel, to listen to your neighbor … to really listen to them?

Notice whether you have good attention as they speak to you … notice how much you yearn to become a better and better listener, not just with your friends but with total strangers …

Now say goodbye to this person … and take a few deep breaths … .

Now picture yourself beginning conversations like this, first once a week, then perhaps a few times a week, until you start feeling so excited about reaching out to your fellow residents that it just becomes natural to you to start conversations as you move through your community doing your errands ...

Now notice that other people in your community, who you have never met, are starting conversations with you, about things that matter to them ... at the post office, on the bus, at work ... Notice how it feels that total strangers are asking you to listen to them ... And your friends and co-workers keep telling you that they're starting to have the same remarkable experience as well. It's starting to have an unexpected and odd effect on what's going on inside of you ...

Something profound is happening where you live ... People who have always felt like strangers are starting to feel like "We." Perhaps you've never quite pictured yourself, your actual self, as an essential part of We the People in the place where you live. But now you are, for the first time. How does that feel? ...

When you start to picture yourself getting more and more engaged with other members of your community, what are the feelings and thoughts that arise in you? ...

[LONG PAUSE]

I invite you to open your eyes ... and to slowly turn your head in one direction, and then the other ... and notice how it feels to see yourself and everyone in your community as if we really are We the People ... because in fact we are. It's not just a nice-sounding phrase, it really is who we are ...

It's time to bring democracy home ... to every city and town ... It's time to dive in deep ... It's time to take great risks, to act with loving boldness ...

We can do this!

Thank you!!

Appendix

About the Author

I was a very intense teenager, growing up in the 1970s in an all-white culturally barren Albuquerque suburb in New Mexico that sprawled endlessly across the desert. Perhaps I was such an intense young person because I was already sensing, clearly enough to be expressing to family and friends, that we were living in an *end-time*. Not in the biblical sense, which I have no real connection with or understanding of, but in the sense of what was already utterly obvious, at least to me, that the entire ecology of Mother Earth was collapsing around me and that people were profoundly alienated, angry, scared, and filled with hopelessness. As a young teen, I could see it on the faces of strangers and on the landscape itself. But there wasn't yet anybody I knew who seemed willing or able to have this difficult conversation with me.

Fortunately for my sanity, I attended one of the most unusual public colleges in the country, The Evergreen State College in Olympia, Washington (1976 to 1981). No grades. No tests. No competition between students. Every student took only one full-time interdisciplinary course per year, most of them taught by a team of professors, each of them from a different academic discipline. My favorite year of college was a full-year course called The Decentralization of Social Systems, where a few dozen of us studied the theory and practice of anarchism. We all worked our asses off, and I was in bliss the entire year.

Another year, I got a semester's full-time credit for going on the 1200-mile Walk For Survival with a few dozen other people (including young children and elders), to bring attention to the soon-to-open Trident Nuclear

Submarine Base at Bangor, Washington, which now hosts the most dangerous and genocidal weapon in the history of the planet. A single submarine captain can launch 408 independently targeted nuclear missiles, each more powerful than the Hiroshima bomb. Pure insanity. And now cruising the world's oceans.

It was in college where I discovered radical feminism, which changed me forever. I will never forget bell hooks' phrase, accurately and scathingly describing our country as a "white supremacist capitalist patriarchy." I was equally inspired by the written words of Susan Griffin, Mary Daly, Adrienne Rich, and Andrea Dworkin.

I led many nonviolent direct action workshops while in college, in preparation for a multi-year campaign to try to stop the construction of the new Trident Nuclear Submarine base at Bangor, Washington and did civil disobedience there thrice. I was also arrested in a five-person civil disobedience action at the maximum security penitentiary in Folsom, California, to bring public attention to a massive hunger strike happening inside the prison that the corporate media wasn't covering, until our arrests.

Evergreen helped me to figure out who I already was and who I wanted to be, the sign of a great college. By the time I graduated, I was already sensing that I would be making a lifelong commitment to becoming a nonviolent social movement revolutionist. Looking back now over so many decades of my blessed life, I have obviously chosen a less traveled path where I have tried my best to live my values every day. To dream into existence the very different world that I have always yearned to live in.

After college, I dove deep into social change organizing and workshop leading. While living in rural Scotland for three years (1982 to 1984), I led dozens of "Despair and Empowerment in the Nuclear Age" workshops across Britain, and co-founded its related social movement there, based primarily on the work of Buddhist scholar Joanna Macy. (More about Joanna in my Dedication.) I also invented and led a new workshop in Britain and the U.S. titled "Active Listening for Activists" as I came to understand that activists tend to be terrible listeners!

Paul Cienfuegos

I lived for five years (1990 to 1995) in a yurt at the edge of the temperate rainforest wilderness of Clayoquot Sound, on the wild west coast of Vancouver Island, Canada, where I played an active role with Friends of Clayoquot Sound in organizing what was at the time the largest sustained nonviolent direct action campaign in Canadian history in 1993, which we named "Clayoquot Summer."

During my final year in Canada, I discovered the groundbreaking work of Richard Grossman who had recently co-founded the Program on Corporations, Law and Democracy (POCLAD.org) to bring much needed and overdue attention to the history of how corporations became such legally powerful institutions in the U.S., and why existing conventional single-issue activism was utterly impotent in challenging corporate power. In what felt like a single mind-shattering flash of a moment, I realized that all of the issues I had ever worked on were mere symptoms of corporate rule, and I quickly pivoted to becoming a trainee in POCLAD's quickly expanding educational efforts. I have been leading related workshops ever since.

Returning to the U.S. in 1995, I co-founded and directed a new organization to model POCLAD's organizing and educational efforts at the local level, Democracy Unlimited of Humboldt County (California). In 1998, I co-directed a ballot initiative campaign in Arcata which succeeded at a local level in beginning to rein in corporate power. It was the first active local effort of its kind in the U.S.. And from that day to this, I have remained laser focused on this very work: dismantling the so-called constitutional "rights" that corporations have been granted by the U.S. Supreme Court beginning in 1819!

Now a leader in what has become known as the community rights movement; giving talks, leading workshops, offering consultations nationwide; I moved to Portland, Oregon in 2011 where I co-founded Community Rights PDX the following year. I co-founded the Oregon Community Rights Network in 2013, and Community Rights US in 2017, which continues to assist communities across the nation.

From 2014 to 2016, I produced a weekly radio commentary and subscribable podcast. (You can access it at https://CommunityRightsUS. podbean.com and clicking on "Weekly Radio Commentary.") David Barsamian's internationally syndicated show Alternative Radio has broadcast many of my speeches.

The community rights movement seeks nothing less than the abolition of corporate rule in this country and the establishment of local communities finally being allowed under law to protect their own health, safety and welfare, freed from a set of ridiculous and patronizing historical legal structures that allow both large corporations and the State to block meaningful participatory democratic change at the local scale.

Working in just one social movement for so many years has been an extraordinary experience, and I have been blessed to have had so many amazing mentors in this work. Most significant among them are Jane Anne Morris who passed in 2019, and Richard Grossman who passed in 2014, both taken from us years before their time.

This is my first book, but likely not my last!

More information about my many workshop offerings, writings, and interviews is at www.CommunityRights.US.

About Community Rights US

Our Mission: To protect the rights of We the People and the natural world by dismantling corporate rule (from the local up)!

At the heart of Community Rights US is the belief that We the People rule over corporate interests because the primary legitimate purpose of law and government is to serve and protect our people, our communities, and nature.

We are a national team of professionals working with communities to pass locally enforceable laws protecting people and nature from destructive corporate practices. We offer continuing support to communities in order to create a sustainable, lasting shift that puts the power back in the hands of the people over the long term.

We provide in-person, phone, and online services to diverse communities working locally to dismantle the structures of law that make destructive corporate practices legal and inevitable, while rediscovering our collective power as "We the People."

Community Rights US facilitates customized support services through a national network of providers addressing the following topics:

- CR education and consulting throughout and beyond ordinance campaign process
- Recognizing CR work within the longer arc of nonviolent social change
- Collaborative decision making
- Paradigm/Consciousness-shifting (learning to respond differently when the legal system tells you "no")
- Working through our grief, sorrow, anger and fear about the state of our society and our world
- Organizing (including meeting facilitation, media & outreach, fundraising, conflict resolution, direct action)

We are a non-profit 501c3 tax-exempt organization, based in Oregon. Our mailing address is: PO Box 86605, Portland, Oregon 97286.

Further Reading

The dozens of essays in this book are a small fraction of public writings that I have done over many decades. It felt important to me to make more of my work available in one place, so I have created a new page on our website, www.CommunityRights.US/Book-More. **Here you will find links to many other essays and speeches, direct access to my more than two years of weekly podcasts, and much much more.**

I encourage you to share my work with others. All I ask is that you contact me in advance of any republishing of my work, so that I can keep track of the widening circles as it moves.

In addition, I want to bring to your attention a list of the core curriculum that the community rights movement uses in our educational work, which can be found at www.CommunityRights.US/Book.

Thank you so much.

Paul Cienfuegos
Paul@CommunityRights.US

Gratitude and Acknowledgments

I offer gratitude to all of my colleagues and allies across the world who helped with editing and reviewing (and just plain nudging) of this, my first-ever published book. I especially wish to thank Evelina Avotina, Caroline Westgate, Stanford Siver, Jim Gurley, Patrick Reinsborough, Matt Nicodemus, Norris Thomlinson, Mark Dilley, Ann Kobsa, Sara Sunstein, Deanna Pumplin, Simon Walter-Hansen, Naga Nataka, Robin Hahnel, Tyler Norman, and Ros Nelson.

My decades of work in the Community Rights movement have been filled with great ups and downs. It is unlikely that I could have survived this many years doing this intensive work without the support and friendship of so many people, especially including: Kelly Brown, Eva Hamilton, Jen Forti, Forest Jahnke, Bryan Lewis, Carla Cao, Michelle Wallar Martin, Cheryle Easter, Steve Luse, Joan Pougiales, Jenny Krol, Heather Tischbein, Curt Hubatch, Deborah Einbender, Mary Thamann, Cindi Fisher, Jocelyn Moore, David Delk, Darla Truitt, Mark Lakeman, Matt Guynn, Treothe Bullock, Cara Cruickshank, Linda Grove, Trisha Mandes, Dean Ritz, Kenya Hart, Jeff Ennor, Amy Greenfield, Lynda McClure, Jan Edwards, Gil Gregori, Ali Boecker, Kelly Larson, Rick Dubrow, Dana Lyons, Kay Firor, Laurence Cole, Jane Anne Morris, Betsy Barnum, Nan Horton, Mike Mertes, Eva Barr, Mary & Jeff Abbas, Sonya Jones, 100 Grannies for a Livable Future, Cheryl Miller, Keith & Virginia Laken, and Medora Woods.

And finally, a deep debt of gratitude to my beloved parents:

- My life-long socialist law professor father Myron who passed away in 2019, and

- My medical social worker mother Elka who only in her last months of life did I finally understand what a deep-community-building powerhouse she was her entire life and who passed away just weeks before I went to press in February 2022.

They were among my biggest fans and I miss them terribly!

Everything gives me hope ... my hope comes from the fact that I know that everybody wants change. I know that people are not apathetic. I know that people are ready for change. I know that alternatives are possible and that you constantly see how hard the establishment has to work to maintain order. Look at all these institutions, the banks of the Thames lined with institutions to hold ordinary people down. Constantly through the media, they try to prevent different arguments emerging. That is because they know change is inevitable.

Change is just a different story. We, people in the media, have an obligation to reframe this argument, to tell people that they can change the world, that we are connected to one another.

We have more in common with each other. We have more in common with the people we're bombing than the people we're bombing them for. People that say the system works work for the system. We can change the world. The revolution can begin as soon as you decide it does in yourself ...

– *Russell Brand*
English comedian, actor, podcast host, author, and activist